ISBN 978-1-332-97313-2
PIBN 10445115

This book is a reproduction of an important historical work. Forgotten Books uses
state-of-the-art technology to digitally reconstruct the work, preserving the original format
whilst repairing imperfections present in the aged copy. In rare cases, an imperfection in
the original, such as a blemish or missing page, may be replicated in our edition. We do,
however, repair the vast majority of imperfections successfully; any imperfections that
remain are intentionally left to preserve the state of such historical works.

English
Français
Deutsche
Italiano
Español
Português

www.forgottenbooks.com

Mythology Photography **Fiction**
Fishing Christianity **Art** Cooking
Essays Buddhism Freemasonry
Medicine **Biology** Music **Ancient**
Egypt Evolution Carpentry Physics
Dance Geology **Mathematics** Fitness
Shakespeare **Folklore** Yoga Marketing
Confidence Immortality Biographies
Poetry **Psychology** Witchcraft
Electronics Chemistry History **Law**
Accounting **Philosophy** Anthropology
Alchemy Drama Quantum Mechanics
Atheism Sexual Health **Ancient History**
Entrepreneurship Languages Sport
Paleontology Needlework Islam
Metaphysics Investment Archaeology
Parenting Statistics Criminology
Motivational

[Coffey, Mr.]

A PRIMER

OF

THE IRISH LANGUAGE,

WITH

COPIOUS READING LESSONS;

FOR THE

USE OF THE STUDENTS

IN

THE COLLEGE OF ST. COLUMBA.

DUBLIN:

HODGES AND SMITH, GRAFTON-STREET,

BOOKSELLERS TO THE UNIVERSITY.

1845.

DUBLIN ·
PRINTED AT THE UNIVERSITY PRESS,
BY M. H. GILL.

PREFACE.

———◆———

THE following Primer was compiled for the use of the junior classes in the College of St. Columba: and it is now published in the hope of removing some of the obstacles which have hitherto opposed the progress of beginners in the Irish language.

It is not intended as a grammar, but rather as a supplement to a grammar; containing progressive lessons in spelling and pronunciation; familiar phrases and sentences; and a useful praxis in reading and translation. The result, it is hoped, will prove acceptable both to teachers and learners, as it is believed that no similar book, calculated for general school purposes, has hitherto existed.

The work would have been made more complete by the insertion of additional spelling lists, including trisyllables and longer words, together with illustrations of the more important Gælic idioms, and rules of construction. But the necessity of a speedy publication rendered it expedient to suspend this part of the plan for the present; and the postponement of it is the less to be regretted, as Mr. O'Donovan's Grammar, now in course of publication at the expense of the College, will afford the means of completing the original design more perfectly, if a second edition of the present work be called for at any future period.

It is necessary to state that the College of St. Columba is indebted for the following work to the joint labours of Mr. Coffey, to whom the department of tuition in the Irish language has been committed, and of the Rev. Robert King. To the latter of these gentlemen are due the original suggestion and plan of the Primer, and particularly the selection and arrangement of the reading Lessons. To Mr. O'Donovan, and the Rev. Dr. Todd, of Trinity College, Dublin, thanks are also due, for the trouble they have taken in reading the proof sheets, and suggesting many useful corrections.

R. C. SINGLETON,
Warden.

Feb. 21, 1845.

CONTENTS.

————◆————

CHAP. I.

OF THE LETTERS IN THEIR SIMPLEST FORMS, ETC.

CHAP. II.

OF ASPIRATION, AND THE CHANGES PRODUCED BY IT IN THE SOUNDS OF THE LETTERS.

CHAP. III.

OF ECLIPSIS.

CHAP. IV.

READING LESSONS.—RELIGIOUS AND MORAL.

CHAP. V.

READING LESSONS, CONSISTING OF SELECT PASSAGES FROM THE HISTORY OF IRELAND BY KEATING.

CHAP. VI.

SACRED LESSONS, CONSISTING OF PASSAGES EXTRACTED FROM THE IRISH VERSION OF THE HOLY SCRIPTURES.

PRIMER OF THE IRISH LANGUAGE.

CHAPTER I.

OF THE LETTERS IN THEIR SIMPLEST FORMS, ETC.

Sect. 1.—*The Alphabet.*

1. The Irish Alphabet consists of eighteen letters, as may be seen in the following Table:

Form.		Names.	Corresponding English Letters.
Capital.	Small.		
A 𝔄	a	ailm	a
B	b	beiꞇh	b
C	c	coll	c
Ꝺ	ꝺ	ꝺuiꞃ	d
E	e	eaꝺha	e
Ꝼ	ꝼ	ꝼeaꞃn	f
Ᵹ	ᵹ	ᵹoꞃꞇ	g
I	ı	ıoᵹha	i
L	l	luiꞅ	l
M	m	muin	m
N	n	nuin	n
O	o	oiꞃ	o
P	p	peiꞇh	p
Ꞃ	ꞃ	ꞃuiꞅ	r
S	ꞅ	ꞅuil	s
Ꞇ	ꞇ	ꞇeine	t
U	u	uꞃ	u
H	h	uaꝺh	h

The Irish names of the letters, although above given for the sake of those who may desire to see them, need not be committed to memory. They all express the names of trees.

2. Table of the most common contractions.

ꝝ or ⁊ (the Latin contraction for *et*) is put for aɡuſ, also for eꞇ and eꝺ.	ꞏ. is put for eaꝺhon, or *id est.*
ᴀ̄ is put for an.	ꝺ̄ ɡan.
4　　　　aſ.	ꞏ ɡuſ.
4̣　　ꞏ aıſ.	ŋ na.
r̄　　achꞇ.	ꞃ̄ nn.
ę　　ea.	ꞅ ſſ.
	ᴋ ſı.
	ꭒ̇ uı.

SECT. 2.—*Of the Sounds of the Vowels and Consonants.*

3. Of the letters as given above, the following seven, viz., b, ꝼ, l, m, n, p, ſ, when in their simplest state, have the same sound as the corresponding English letters.

4. c and ɡ are always sounded hard ; c as in the English word *come*, or like the *k* in *king;* never soft, as the *c* in *city, cedar*, &c. ɡ answers to the sound of the corresponding English letter in *gone* or *guile:* it is never soft, as in *ginger.*

5. ꝺ and ꞇ have each of them a twofold sound, viz., ꝺ sounds either as *th* in the English words, *there, this ;* or as an English *d* accompanied with a slender sound of the letter *y.* In like manner ꞇ (when followed by a broad vowel) is sounded either as the *th* in *thick*, or as an English *t*, accompanied by the same slender sound of *y.*

The nearest approach in English words to the last mentioned sounds of ꝺ and ꞇ is perhaps that which occurs in the words *Indian, fustian*, &c. Observe, however, that there is in these words respectively, a sound of *g* soft, and *ch*, which does not belong to the Irish letters here spoken of, and which must therefore be cárefully avoided in the pronunciation of them.

6. ſ has a two-fold power; sounding in some places as the simple *s* in the English word *same;* in other places like *sh* in *shine.*—(See No. 8.)

7. The vowels, as in English, are five in number; they are divided into two classes, *broad* and *slender.* There are three broad, viz., α, o, u, and two slender, viz., e and ı.

8. The letters o, ꞇ, ſ, when connected with broad vowels, have the first sounds assigned to them in the preceding remarks (Nos. 5 and 6). When connected with slender vowels, they have the second sounds there assigned to them.

9. Each of the vowels has a long sound in some places, thus:

α in báſ, bán, is sounded like the English *a* in *call.*
e in lén, ſe . . . . *e* in *they.*
ı in mín (*smooth*), nı, ... *ee* in *been.*
o in móp, óᵹ, ... *o* in *gold.*
u in cú, ꞇú, ... *u* in *rule.*

10. The long vowels are commonly marked with an accent, drawn from right to left, which is peculiar to them, and is the only accent used in writing Irish, thus: báſ, *death.*

11. Each of the vowels has also one or more short sounds, as follows:

α in αlꞇ, is sounded like the English *a* in *what.*
– in ꞇαp, ... *a* in *hat.*
e in ſel, ... *e* in *sell.*
ı in mın (*meal*), ... *i* in *pit.*
o in olꞇ, ... *o* in *work.*
u in oul, ... *u* in *sun.*
– in puſ, ... *u* in *pull.*

12. The vowels (as is the case in every language) have also occasionally an obscure or indistinct sound, of which the following are instances;

ɑ in ꞇuꞃɑ, póꞃꞇɑ, is sounded like *a* in *funeral*.

e in mɩlꞃe, ꝋíle, ... *e* in *manner*.

13. Finally, in some positions, ɑ and o have a very peculiar sound, answering to that of the *i* in *wide;* this will be more fully explained hereafter.

Sᴇᴄᴛ. 3.—*Spelling Exercises on the preceding Rules.*

14. Monosyllables.

ál, a clutch.	ꝋɑll, blind.
ɑnn, there.	ꝋán, a poem.
áꞃ, slaughter.	ꝼá, under, about.
áꝑꝋ, a height.	ꝼáᵹ, leave.
báꝋ, a boat.	ᵹɑnn, scarce.
bɑll, a spot, a limb.	lá, a day.
bán, white.	lán, full.
báꝑꝋ, a poet.	láꞃ, middle.
báꞃ, death.	má, if.
cá, where.	mám, handful.
cláꞃ, a board.	ná, nor.
ꝋá, if, two.	ꝑꞃáꞃ, brass.

15. ꞃál, a heel.	cɑm, crooked.
ꞃáꞃ, excellent.	cɑꞃ, twist.
ꞃlán, sound, whole.	cɑꞇ, a cat.
ꞇá, is.	cꞃɑnn, a tree.
ꞇɑll, beyond, over.	ꝋɑꞃꞇ, a clod.
ꞇán, time.	ꝼɑꝋ, length, whilst.
ɑlꞇ, a joint.	ᵹɑl, vapour.
ɑm, time.	ᵹɑn, without.
bɑ, cows.	ᵹɑꞃ, near, advantage.
bɑꞃ, palm of the hand.	ᵹɑꞃ, stalk.
blɑꞃ, taste.	ᵹlɑc, take.
cɑꝋ, what.	ᵹlɑn, clean.

16. glas, green.
lag, weak.
las, light (*verb*).
mac, a son.
mar, as.
rann, a verse.
ralt, a leap.
slat, a rod.
ab, a father.
ag, with.
an, the.
ar, our.
as, out of.
brat, a garment.
tar, come.
tart, thirst.
cé, who.
gné, kind, form.
é, he, it.
lé, with.
lén, woe.
mé, I, me.
ré, with.
sé, six.

17. sé, he, six.
té, a person.
tré, through.
fel, strife.
bí, be thou.
dím, from me, of me.
í, she, it.
ím, butter.
lín, flax, a line.
mí, a month.
mín, smooth.
ní, not.
sí, she.
tí, a person.
tír, country.
trí, three.
tríd, through.
glic, wise.
is, is.
mil, honey.
min, meal.
ris, with him.
sin, that.
sinn, we.

18. tig, come.
bó, a cow.
bórd, a table.
bróg, a shoe.
brón, grief.
cró, a hovel.
dó, two.
fód, a sod.
fós, yet.
glór, voice.
mór, great.
nó, or.
nós, manner.
óg, young
ól, drink (*verb*).
ór, gold.
póg, a kiss.
pór, seed.
soc, a ploughshare.
ró, very.
ród, a passage.
bog, soft.
clog, a bell.
cnoc, a hill.

19. corp, a body.
cos, the foot.
do, thy.
donn, brown.

ʒo, until, that.
ʒob, a beak.
ʒol, crying.
ʒoꞃm, blue.
ʒoꞃꞇ, field.
ʒꞃou, quick.
lonʒ, ship.
loꞃʒ, footstep.
mo, my.
olc, evil.

20. ꞇꞃom, heavy.
ꞇꞃoꞃʒ, a codfish.
cꞃúb, a paw.
cú, a hound.
cúl, the back.
oún, a fort.
ʒlún, a knee.
púnꞇ, a pound.
ꞃúʒ, a wrinkle.
ꞃún, a secret.
ꞃúo, or úo, yonder.
ꞇú, thou.

21. Dissyllables.
aca, with them.
aʒa, with whom.
aʒao, with thee.
aʒam, with me.
aʒuꞃ, and.
allóo, formerly.
anál, breath.
anall, hither.
anam, soul.
ané, yesterday.
anꞃó, woe.
annꞃa, in the.

22. baꞇa, a stick.
bꞃaoán, a salmon.

oꞃm, upon me.
oꞃꞇ, on thee.
poll, a hole, a pit.
poꞃꞇ, a tune.
ꞃoꞃʒ, an eye.
ꞃo, this.
ꞃon, sake.
ꞇoll, pierce.
ꞇonn, a wave.
ꞇoꞃo, silence.

ꞇúꞃ, beginning.
úꞃ, fresh.
bun, root, bottom.
cum, shape.
cuꞃ, power.
oul, going.
ʒuꞃ, that (*conj.*)
muc, a pig.
pluc, a cheek.
puꞃ, a lip.
ꞃuʒ, brought.
ꞃul, before.

annꞃin, there.
annꞃo, here.
annꞃa, beloved.
an ꞇ-am, } when.
an ꞇan, }
apꞃꞇol, an apostle.
aꞃán, bread.
apíꞃ, again.
aꞃao, out of thee.
aꞃal, an ass.
baʒún, bacon.
balla, a wall.

cꞃúꞃʒa, a jar.
caꞃall, a horse.

cαρα, a friend.
cαρbαꝺ, a carriage.
cαρρán, a reaping-hook.
cáραn, a path.
cαρóᵹ, a coat.
cαρτα, twisted.
cαρúρ, a hammer.
cιρꝺe, treasure.
clαmραρ, strife.
cnocán, a hillock.
coᵹαρ, whisper.

colαm, a dove.
colαnn, the body.
coρcán, a small pot.
cuꝺóᵹ, a haddock.
cumα, indifferent.
cupán, a cup.
ꝺánα, bold, impudent.
ꝺαρα, second.
ꝺíle, a deluge.
ꝺonαρ, misfortune.
ꝺoρuρ, a door.

23. ραꝺα, long.
ριle, a poet.
ρocαl, a word.
ρollαρ, manifest.
ρoναρ, knowledge.
ρuναρ, easy.
ᵹαlαρ, a disease.
ᵹαρρún, a lad.
ᵹαρτα, brisk.
ᵹonτα, wounded.
h-αllα, a hall.
h-ατα, a hat.
ιnᵹne, nails, claws.

ιnιρ, an island.
ιnnτιnn, the mind.
lαρτα, lighted.
lαρóᵹ, a blaze.
lιτιρ, a letter.
míle, a mile, a thousand.
mιlιρ, sweet.
mιlρe, sweetness.
míne, smoothness.
mιnιc, frequent.
mιρe, I myself.
míρe, madness.
molτα, praised.

24. móρán, much.
munα, unless.
noρα, custom.
obαnn, sudden.
ocραρ, hunger.
olα, oil.
olαnn, wool.
oρꝺóᵹ, a thumb.
oραρ, junior.
oρcαρ, the arm.
ραρluρ, a parlour.
pobαl, people.

poρτán, a crabfish.
póρτα, married.
poτα, a pot.
puναnn, a sheaf.
puτóᵹ, a pudding.
ραρán, a shrubbery.
ριbe, a hair.
ραᵹαρτ, a priest.
ραlαnn, salt.
ráρτα, satisfied.
ρᵹαꝺán, a herring.
ρᵹιlιnᵹ, a shilling.

25. ρᵹolóᵹ, a farmer.
ρmιᵹín, the chin.

ρoꝺαρ, trotting.
ρolαρ, light.

롤áp, comfort.
ᵱonaᵱ, happiness.
ᵱpapán, a purse.
ᵱponóᴣ, a spoon.
ᵱuᴅóᴣ, a cake.
ᵱuᴣán, a straw rope.
ᴛamall, awhile.
ᴛıᵱım, dry.
ᴛobaᵱ, a well.
ᴛollᴛa, pierced.
ᴛoᵱann, a noise.

ᴛoᵱaᵱ, a journey.
ᴛúᵱna, a spinning-wheel.
ᴛuᵱa, thyself.
ᴛuᵱlóᴣ, a leap.
ᴛuᵱlonᴣ, breakfast.
umaᴅ, about thee.
úmal, obedient.
umpa, about them.
úᵱlán, very full.
uᵱlán, } a floor.
oᵱlán, }

Sect. 4.—*Sounds of the long Diphthongs, and Spelling Exercises on them.*

26. There are in Irish thirteen diphthongs, viz., ae, aı, ao, ea, eı, eo, eu, ıa, ıo, ıu, oı, ua, uı; of which the following five, viz., ae, ao, eu, ıa, ua, are always long. The remaining eight are sometimes long and sometimes short.

27. Diphthongs having their first vowel long are generally pronounced like dissyllables, thus: ᴛaım, ᵱuaᵱ, ᴣᵱıan, are faintly sounded, as if they were written ᴛa-ım ᵱu-aᵱ, ᴣᵱı-an.

28. No vowels in Irish are doubled like those in the English words *poor, green,* &c. Nor are any final vowels suppressed in pronunciation, as those in the English words *hate, strike,* &c., the Irish words ᴅıle, mıᵱe, ᵱınce, &c., being dissyllables.

29. The sounds of the five long diphthongs may be represented in English as follows:

ae sounds like *ai* in *pain,* as lae, *of a day.*

ao . . . . *ea* in *tear,* as ᵱaoᵱ, *cheap.*

eu . . . . *ayo* in *mayor,* as ᴣeuᵱ, *sharp.*

ıa . . . . *ee* in *seer,* as cıall, *sense.*

ua . . . . *ua* in *truant,* as ᵱuaᵱ, *cold.*

30. Spelling exercises on the long diphthongs.

aeρ, the sky.	cρeuᴏ, what.
aeρ, an age.	ꝼeuρ, grass.
lae, of a day.	ʒeuʒ, a branch.
ρe, the moon.	ʒeuρ, sour.
aol, lime.	meuρ, a finger.
aon, one.	neul, a cloud.
blaoρʒ, husk.	ρaob, a rent.
bρaon, a drop	ρeulᴄ, a star.
caol, slender.	ρeun, prosperity.
ᴏaoρ, dear.	ρʒeul, a story.
maol, bald.	ρρeuρ, the firmament.
ρaoρ, cheap.	ᴄρeuᴏ, a flock.
beul, the mouth.	ciall, sense.

31.
cian, far, distant.	buan, lasting.
ᴏiaρ, two.	cuan, a bay.
ʒiall, the jaw.	cluaρ, an ear.
ʒρian, the sun.	cρuaρ, hardness.
iaᴏ, they.	ᴏual, duty.
iaρ, after.	ᴏuan, a poem.
iaρʒ, a fish.	ꝼuaρ, cold.
mian, desire.	ʒρuaʒ, hair.
ρian, pain.	ʒual, coal.
ρiaρᴄ, a worm.	ρcuab, a broom.
ρʒian, a knife.	ρuan, sleep.
ρiaρ, west.	ρuaρ, up.
ρliaρ, the thigh.	ua, a grandson.
ρρian, a rein.	uan, a lamb.

SECT. 5.—*Sounds of the variable Diphthongs, with Spelling Exercises on them.*

32. The sounds of the variable diphthongs may be nearly represented in English as follows ·

1°. ai long, sounds like *awi* in *drawing*, as ᴄáim, *I am.*

ai short, . . . *a* in *fang*, as ρail, *a willow.*

or like *i* in *calling*, as laρaip, *a light.*

and sometimes, but seldom, as *e* in *herd*, thus, aiρ, *upon.*

2°. eα long, sounds as *a* in *care*, thus, ſméaſ, *a blackberry.*

eα short, . . *ea* in *heart*, . . ceaſc, *right.*

It is also sometimes obscure.—(See *Chap.* II. *Sect.* 1.)

3°. eı long, sounds as *ei* in *reign*, thus, ſéın, *self.*

eı short, sounds like *e* in *wreck*, . . leıſ, *with him.*

4°. eo long, sounds like *yeo* in *yeoman*, thus, ceól, *music.*

eo short . . . *you* in *young*, . . ſeo, *this.*

5°. ıo long, sounds as *ee* in *seer*, thus, ſíon, *wine.*

ıo short, . . . *i* in *mill*,˙ ſıoſ, *knowledge.*

6°. ıu long, sounds like *u* in *true*, as ſcıúſ, *a helm.*

ıu short, . . . *u* in *young*, as ſıum, *with me.*

7°. oı long, sounds as *oi* in *going*, as cóıſ, *just.*

or as *i* in *mile*, as coıll, *a wood.*

oı short, sounds like *ui* in *quill*, as coıſ, *a crime.*

seldom like *ea* in *head*, as cſoıo, *a fight.*

8°. uı long, sounds as *ui* in *ruin*, so cúıჳ, *five.*

uı short, . . . *ui* in *quill*, thus, ſuıl, *blood.*

33. It is to be observed, that in some parts of Ireland the diphthong eα short, and also the long α, are in some words pronounced nearly like *ow* in *fowl*: thus, ceann, ჳleann, báll, ám, are pronounced in those places *keown, gloun, boul, oum ;* but this pronunciation seems altogether improper, and should be carefully avoided.

34. It is also to be here observed, that the letters b, ſ, m, combined with uı, or αoı coming after them, are always sounded like *bw, fw, mw*: as ſuıl (*fwill*), *blood;* muıſ (*mwirr*), *the sea;* baoıſ (*bweesh*), *folly;* ſαoı (*fwee*), *under;* mαoın (*mween*), *property.*

35. Spelling exercises on the variable diphthongs.

αıll, a cliff.	cáıc, where.
áıc, a place.	cnáıb, hemp.
cáın, a fine.	cſáın, a sow.
cαıll, a name.	ſáıl, a ring.

páirc, a field.
páirt, a part.
raint, covetousness.
rġáil, a shadow.
rráid, a street.
táir, thou art.
air, backwards.
ait, pleasant.
bail, prosperity.
cailc, chalk.

caint, talk.
dair, an oak.
dairt, a clod.
rail, a beam.
rtair, a history.
air, upon.
braon, a drop.
bréaġ, a lie.
céad, a hundred; first.
céard, a trade.

---

36. déan, make or do.
   déar, a tear.
   éad, jealousy.
   éaġ, death.
   éan, a bird.
   léan, misery.
   méad, quantity.
   réan, deny.
   rméar, blackberry.
   téad, a rope.
   trear, third.
   bean, a woman.
   breac, speckled.
   cead, permission.

ceann, a head.
ceap, a last.
cearc, a hen.
ceart, right.
clear, a game, play.
dealġ, a thorn.
dearġ, red.
dear, nice.
dream, people.
fead, a whistle.
fear, a man.
fearġ, anger.
ġeal, white.
ġean, love.

---

37. leat, with you.
   mear, swift, active.
   meas, estimation.
   measġ, mix.
   nead, a nest.
   neart, strength.
   peann, a pen.
   rean, old.
   rearc, love.
   rear, stand.
   rpeal, a scythe.
   tear, heat.
   béic, a cry.
   béim, a blow.
   céir, wax.

cléir, the clergy.
céir, a sow.
déirc, alms.
éirt, listen.
féil, a feast.
ġéir, a swan.
léir, the whole.
léiġ, let.
méid, bulk.
réir, last night.
beirt, two.
ceir, a basket.
ceirt, a question.
cleit, a feather.
creid, believe.

38. ᵹeın, beget.
    leıꞃ, with him.
    ꞃeıc, sell thou.
    beó, alive.
    ceó, a fog.
    ceól, music.
    ഠeóꞃ, a tear.
    leó, with them.
    leóꞃ, enough.
    ꞃeo, this.
    cíoꞃ, a comb.
    cíoꞃ, rent.
    cꞃíon, withered.

    ഠíol, pay.
    ഠíom, from me.
    ꝼíon, wine.
    ꝼíoꞃ, true.
    íoc, rent, payment.
    líon, fill.
    píob, a pipe.
    ꞃcꞃíob, a scratch.
    ꞃíol, seed.
    ꞃíoꞃ, down.
    bıoꞃ, a spit.
    cıon, love.
    cꞃıoꞃ, a girdle.

39. ꝼıonn, fair.
    ꝼıoꞃ, knowledge.
    lıom, with me.
    lıoꞃ, a fort.
    ꞃıoc, with thee.
    ꞃᵹꞃıoꞃ, destruction.
    ꞃıoc, frost.
    ഠıúl, sucking.
    ꝼıú, worthy.
    ıúl, knowledge.
    ꞃıú, with them.
    ꞃıúꞃ, a sister.
    ꞃcıúꞃ, a helm.
    ꞇꞃıúꞃ, three persons.

    cóıꞃ, right.
    ꝼóıl, a while.
    ᵹlóıꞃ, glory.
    móıഠ, a vow.
    móın, turf.
    nóın, evening.
    ꞇóıꞃ, search.
    ꞇóıꞇ, smoke.
    coıll, a wood.
    moıll, delay.
    ꞃoınn, portion.
    coıꞃ, a crime.
    ᵹoıഠ, theft.
    ᵹoıꞃ, call.

40. loıꞇ, wound.
    ꞇoıl, will.
    ꞇoıꞃꞇ, bulk.
    oıl, nurture.
    oıꞃ, east.
    ꞃꞇoıꞃm, a storm.
    ꞇꞃoıഠ, a fight.
    cúıᵹ, five.
    cúıꞃ, cause.
    ഠúıl, desire.
    ഠúınn, to us.

    ꞃúıl, an eye.
    ꞃúıꞃꞇ, a flail.
    ꞇúıꞃ, incense.
    buılᵹ, bellows.
    cluın, hear.
    cꞃuıꞇ, a harp.
    cuıഠ, a part.
    cuıꞃ, put.
    ഠꞃuıഠ, shut.
    ഠꞃuım, the back.
    ഠuın an oak.

ouιτ, to thee.
puιl, blood.
muιp, the sea.

pluιo, a blanket.
τuιτ, a fall.

SECT. 6.—*Of the Triphthongs, and Spelling Exercises on them.*

41. There are in Irish five triphthongs, viz., aoι, eoι, ιaι, ιuι, and uaι, which are always long. The following table exhibits the sounds corresponding to them in English.

aoι answers to *ee* in *keep,* as in aoιp, *age.*
eoι *yeo* in *yeoman, with i after it,* as peoιl, *flesh.*
ιaι . *eei* in *seeing,* as in oιaιl, *a dial.*
ιuι . *iewi* in *viewing,* as in cιuιn, *mild.*
uaι *ui* in *ruin,* as in cuaιpτ, *a visit.*
or sometimes as *i* in *dine,* so uaιτ, *from thee.*

42. Spelling exercises.

aoι, an island.
aoιp, age.
baoιp, folly.
caoι, method.
caoιl, the waist.
caoιn, gentle.
cuaoι, consumption.
opaoι, a druid.
paoι, under.
zaoιl, kindred.
maoιl, a heap.
maoιn, wealth.
naoι, nine.
beoιp, beer.
ceoιl, songs.
eoιnn, birds.
peoιl, flesh.

peoιo, jewels.
peoιl, sails.
τpeoιp, a guide.
bιaιl, an axe.
oιaιl, a dial.
cιuιn, mild.
buaιl, strike.
buaιn, reaping.
buaιpτ, affliction.
cluaιn, a plain.
puaιm, a sound.
puaιp, found.
zuaιp, danger.
uaιm, from me.
uaιn, time.
uaιp, an hour.
uaιτ, from thee.

c

SECT. 7.—*Spelling Exercises on the Diphthongs. Dissyllables.*

43. Dissyllables with one diphthong.

abaıp, say.
aıce, with her.
aıcıo, disease.
aıӡe, with him.
aıpe, care.
aımpıp, time.
aıplınӡ, a vision.
áluınn, handsome.
baıle, a town.
baıne, milk.
baınıp, a wedding.
bıolap, cresses.
bıopán, a pin.
bpıonӡlóo, a vision.
buılín, a loaf.

caılín, a girl.
cappaıc, a rock.
céıle, together, a spouse.
cıonup, how.
cíonóӡ, a very small coin.
coınín, a rabbit.
coıpce, oats.
copcéım, a footstep.
cpeıoım, I believe.
cpıona, wise.
oeapmao, forgetfulness.
oeıfıp, haste.
ouılle, a leaf.
ouıne, a man.
éaoan, the face.

44. eaӡna, wisdom.
eapboӡ, a bishop.
eıle, other.
eólup, knowledge.
fáıne, a ring.
faıppӡe, the sea.
faıppınӡ, wide.
fallaınӡ, a cloak.
feapann, land.
féapóӡ, the beard.
féıoıp, ability.
popӡaıl, open (*verb*).
fneaӡpa, an answer.
ӡaıle, the stomach.
ӡeappan, a hack horse.
ӡıolla, a servant.

ӡlıocap, prudence.
ӡloıne, a glass.
ӡuala, a shoulder.
ıomao, much.
ıonӡa, a nail.
láıoıp, strong.
lapaıp, a light.
leanaım, I follow.
léıne, a shirt.
léıpӡe, laziness.
maıoe, a stick.
maıoın, a morning.
maılle, with.
meacan, a carrot, parsnip, &c.

45. mioltóg, a midge.
muinntir, people.
náire, shame.
nóinín, a daisy.
obair, a work.
óige, youth.
pairoe, a child.
pioppa, a pear.
píora, a piece.
póipín, a small potato.
peilig, a churchyard.
rzioból, a barn.
riopa, a shop.
rláinte, health.
rlaooán, a cough.
rleagán, a shell.

rloine, a sirname.
rluarao, a shovel.
rocaip, quiet.
rpioeóg, a nightingale.
rpíonann, a gooseberry bush.
rpíopao, a spirit.
teagarg, teaching.
teampoll, a church. ——
teanga, a tongue.
tiomna, a will.
tinntean, a hearth.
tuile, a flood, more.
tuigre, understanding.
uaral, noble.
uirge, water.

---

46. Dissyllables with two diphthongs.

aingeal, an angel.
airgioo, silver, money.
airnéir, cattle, furniture.
buioeal, a bottle.
caipoear, friendship.
cairleán, a castle.
coinneal, a candle.
coinleoir, a candlestick.
cpoiceann, the skin.
cuileóg, a fly.
cuinneóg, a churn.
oeacair, difficult.
ooinean, foul weather.
eaglair, a church.

fuineóg, a window.
muineal, the neck.
oineao, so much.
páipeir, paper.
reanmóir, a sermon.
réipéal, a chapel.
rzpiobtúir, scripture.
roinean, fine weather.
roirgéul, the gospel.
ruipéar, supper.
toipmearg, hindrance.
tpionóio, the Trinity.
uillean, an elbow.
uireóg, a lark.

SECT. 8.—*Short Phrases and Sentences.*

47. cia ſin?   Who is that?

    ᵹo oé ſin?   What is that?

    ᵹo ɼin opc?   What ails you?

    ſonaſ opc.   Good fortune to you.

    ſlán leac.   Good bye to you.

    oéan oeiſiſ.   Make haste.

    caſ anioſ.   Come up.

    ciᵹ aiſ aiſ.   Come back.

    na bſiſ é.   Do not break it.

    beiſ leac é.   Take it with you.

    an ſíoſ ſin?   Is that true?

    ca me ſaſoa.   I am satisfied.

    ca ſe ſlan.   He is well.

    na cſeio é.   Do not believe it (or him.)

---

48. ᵹo oé an uaiſ.   · What is the hour?

    ca ſé mall.   It is late.

    ſan ᵹo ſocaiſ.   Stay quietly.

    iſ éiᵹin oom.   I must.

    caſ anaice liom.   Come near me.

    ca ſé aᵹam.   I have it.

    ca ſé uaim.   I want it.

    na oéan oeaſmao.   Do not forget.

    ca eaᵹla oſm.   I am afraid.

    iſ coil liom.   I wish.

    ma 'ſ coil leac.   If you wish.

    ca ſeaſᵹ aiſ.   He is angry.

---

49. ca h-aoiſ ouic?   What is your age?

    na h-abaiſ ſin.   Do not say that.

an aıl leaꞇ é?	Do you like it.
nı h-aıl lıom é.	I do not like it.
ꝼan lıom ꞇamall.	Wait a while for me.
ꝼoꞃꞅaıl an ꝺoꝛuꞃ.	Open the door.
ꝺꞃuıꝺ an ꝺoꝛuꞃ.	Shut the door.
ꞇa ꞇaꝑꞇ oꞃm.	I am thirsty.
ꞃéıꝺ an ꞇeıne.	Blow the fire.
ꞃuꞃ ꞃe leıꞃ é.	He took it with him.
ꞇa cıon aꞅam oꞃꞇ.	I am fond of you.
ꞇa eóluꞃ aꞅam aıꞃ.	I know it (or *him.*)

---

50. céaꝺ míle ꝼáılꞇe.	A hundred thousand welcomes.
ca ꝼaꝺ aꞃ ꞃo é?	How far is it from this?
ıꞃ cuma lıom ꞃın.	That is little matter to me.
ꞇáım aꞅ ꝺul anoıꞃ.	I am going now.
ꞇa ꞃe aꞅ ꞃıoc.	It is freezing.
caꝺ ıꞃ aınm ꝺuıꞇ?	What is your name?
caꝺ ꝺo ꝛınne ꞇu?	What have you done?
ꝺéan ꞃın ꞅo ceaꝑꞇ.	Do that rightly.
ꞇa ꝺúıl aꞅam ann.	I have a desire for it.
ıꞃ ꞃo aıꞇ lıom é.	I like it very much.
cıonaꞃ ꞇá ꞃe anoıꞃ?	How is he now?
ꞇa ꞃe níoꞃ ꝼeaꞃꞃ.	He is better.

---

51. an ı ꞃo ꝺo ꞃꞅıanꞃa?	Is this your knife?
meaꞃaım ꞅuꞃ b'e.	I think it is [or, that it is *he.*]
cía aꞃ leıꞃ an maıꝺe ꞃo?	Whose is this stick?
ıꞃ lıom ꝼéın é.	It is my own.
cıa b'e le'ꞃ mıan é.	Whoever has a mind.
cuıꞃꝼaꝺ ꝼıoꞃ aıꞃ.	I will send for him.

c 2

véanfav ma'f féioip.	I will do it if possible.
nil neapt aɤam aip.	I cannot help it.
cuip opt vo h-ata.	Put on your hat.
ɤeapp apán ir im.	Cut bread and butter.
cinnur tá tu.	How are you ?
fan annpin ɤo fóil.	Stay there awhile.

---

52. nil veifip móp opm.	I am in no great hurry.
ni fiu biopán e.	It is not worth a pin.
cia h-i an cailín pin ?	Who is that girl ?
cia h-iav na vaoinere ?	Who are these people ?
ir liompa e pin.	That is mine.
an é pin é ?	Is that it ?
ni hé pin é.	That is not it.
an meapan tu map pin ?	Do you think so ?
ni abpaim níor mó.	I say no more.
má tá re map a veip tu.	If it be as you say.
cpéuv ir ciall ve pin ?	What is the meaning of that ?
ir láioip an feap é.	He is a strong man.
ir vear an cailin i pin.	That is a nice girl.
an mían leat ɤloine fiona ?	Do you wish for a glass of wine ?

---

53. cpév fá a pinne tu pin ?	Why did you do that ?
na rear eavpom 'ra teine.	Do not stand between me and the fire.
nil aon-vuine ann pin.	There is no person there.
ir ɤlic na vaoine iav.	They are sensible people.
ir vaoine ɤlioca iav.	They are sensible people.
tóɤ leat é aɤur fáil-te.	Take it with you and welcome.

τα ρε 'n αm ρροιnne.	It is dinner time.
τα ʒo leóρ αʒαm ve.	I have enough of it.
ιρ ʒéuρ αn ρʒían ι ρo.	This is a sharp knife.
τα me αρ αnαιl ʒo h-ιomlán.	I am quite out of breath.
ριnne ρe mαρ ριn.	He did so.
ιρ olc αn αιmριρ ι ρo.	This is bad weather.

---

54. ιρ ριne é nα mιρe. — He is older than I.

ιρ eιριon αn τé ιρ óιʒe αcα. — He is the youngest of them.

'ρι αn τí ιρ veιρe αcα. — She is the nicest of them.

ιρ ρolluρ ʒuρ ρeαρ cóιρ é. — It is evident that he is an upright man.

cuιρ αn coιρe αιρ α τeιne. — Put the kettle on the fire.

cιonαρ τα ριαv ʒo h-uιle ? — How are they all ?

cαv ιρ αιnm ve 'n αιτ ρo ? — What is the name of this place ?

cαv ρá αρ leιʒ τu uαιτ é ? — Why did you let him go from you ?

ʒo ve ιαρραρ τu αιρ ρo ? — What do you ask for this ?

ʒo ve αρ ιoc τu αιρ ? — What did you pay for it ?

α ρuʒ τu αn bαιne leατ? Ruʒαρ. — Did you bring the milk ? I did.

'ρe ρo αn ραvv α veιρ ρe. — This is what he says.

CHAPTER II.

OF ASPIRATION, AND THE CHANGES PRODUCED BY IT IN THE
SOUNDS OF THE LETTERS.

———

SECT. 1.—*Of the Sounds of Aspirated Letters.*

55. The letters b, c, ꜱ, ꝼ, ᵹ, m, p, ꞃ, ꞇ, are called *muta-ble* consonants, from the complete change or loss of their original sounds which they suffer in certain positions. The alterations thus introduced are effected in a two-fold man-ner, viz., either by aspiration or eclipsis : the former of these we shall now consider.

56. A consonant is said to be aspirated when the change of sound is indicated by a dot placed over it, thus ḃ, ċ, ḋ, &c. ; or by the letter h written after it.   The powers of the aspirated letters are as follows :

57. ḃ and ṁ joined with *broad* vowels, in the beginning and middle of words, have generally the sound of *w*, as mo baꝺ, *my boat*, pronounced *mo waudh ;* labꞃaim (*lowrim*), *I speak ;* mo ṁac (*mŏ wŏc*), *my son ;* aṁáin (*awauin*), *alone.*

The same letters, when connected with slender vowels, or at the end of words, sound for the most part like *v ;* as biꝺaꞃ (*veedhar*), *they were ;* ꞃliab (*shleeuv*), *a mountain ;* mo ṁeuꞃ (*mo vēur*), *my finger ;* laiṁ (*lawiv*), *of a hand.*

58. ṁ is often silent in the middle of words, especially in the preposition coṁ, as coṁaꞃꞃa (*cō-ărsă*), *a neighbour :* at the end of words after a broad vowel it has a peculiar

sound like that of *w*, followed by a very slender sound of
v, as nαoṁ (*neeow'v*), *a saint;* lαṁ (*law'v*), *a hand.*

59. ċ before or after a broad vowel has the rough sound
of *gh* in *lough;* as luċ (*lugh*), *a mouse;* mo ċoɼ (*mŏ ghus*),
my foot.

ċ connected with a slender vowel is little more than a
strong aspirate sound ; as ċɪm (*heem*), *I see;* mo ċeαn
(*mŏgh-yan*), *my head;* ᴠeɪċ (*dyeh*), *ten.*

60. ὁ and ᵹ̇ in the beginning of a word or syllable, followed by a broad vowel, have a peculiar sound to which
there is no equivalent in English. The nearest approach
to it may be found in the strong guttural sound of *gh*, followed by a slight sound of *w* in some cases, as mo ᵹ̇oɼᴇ
(pronounced somewhat like *mŏgh-worth*), *my field;* mo ὁun
(*mogh woon*), *my fort.*

ὁ and ᵹ̇ in the beginning of words connected with small
vowels, have the sound of the consonant *y;* as ɼo ὁeαɼ,
very nice, pronounced *ro yas;* mo ᵹ̇ɪollα (*mo yilla*), *my
servant.*

61. In the middle and end of words these two aspirated
letters are not sounded as consonants ; but either serve
merely to modify the sounds of vowel combinations, or else
are entirely suppressed in the pronunciation.

αὁ in the beginning of uncompounded words before a
broad vowel, or before the letters l, n, ɼ, and ᵹ, sounds like
the English *i* in *mine.* Thus αὁαɼc, *a horn,* is pronounced
ĭ-urk; ɼαὁαɼc, *sight,* pronounced *ri-urk;* and so αὁɼαɪm
(*i-rum*), *I adore;* αὁlαcαɪm (*ilakim*), *I bury;* ᴛαὁᵹ (*Thĭg*),
Teigue or Thady.

62. oὁ is sometimes similarly pronounced; as oὁαn (*ĭan*),
a caldron.

63. αὁ ending in a word has the obscure sound of *a* in
general; as bαlαὁ, *a smell,* pronounced *bollă;* ᵹeαɼɼαὁ

(*garra*), *cutting:* eaó sounds like *ew* in *sinew*, as pinneaó, *was made*, pronounced (*rin-you*).

64. In such instances as the following, ó and ᵹ̇ are altogether silent: piaónuipe, *witness*, pronounced *fee-a-nishĕ;* paió (*faw-ee*), *a prophet;* bióim (*bee-im*), *I am usually;* ciᵹ̇eapna (*thee-ăr-na*), *a lord;* piᵹ̇ (*ree*), *a king;* amuiᵹ̇ (*am-wee*), *out;* puiᵹe (*seeya*), *sitting;* cpoióe (*kree*), *the heart;* buióe (*bwee*), *yellow;* plánuᵹaó (*slau-noo*), *salvation;* the termination uᵹaó being little more in sound than a lengthened *u*.

65. aᵹaió, *the face*, is pronounced like the English word *eye:* this is in accordance with the preceding observations, for the word, though always spelt with a ᵹ̇, must have been originally aóaió, as appears from the analogy of other languages, (Greek εἶδος), &c.

66. ḟ is altogether silent, as an ḟeile, *the festival*, pronounced *an ay-lă*.

67. ṗ has the sound of *ph* or *f*, as mo ṗup, *my lip*, pronounced *mo foŏs*.

68. ḟ and ċ always sound like *h*, as a ḟal, *his heel*, pronounced *a hall;* mo ċiᵹ̇eapna (*mo heerna*), *my lord*.

68. No primitive words in Irish are found to contain ṗ or ḟ; although some words introduced from other languages are improperly spelt with ṗ, as Phaipipineaċ, *a Pharisee*, &c.; these words ought to be written with an p. The error of the former method appears plainly in the vocatives of these words, in which the first consonant is completely silent, they being pronounced as if written with ph, as a Fhaipipiniᵹ̇.

Sect. 2.—*Spelling Exercises on the Aspirates.*

70. Monosyllables.

balḃ, dumb.
ḃí, was.
cnaoḃ, a branch.
duḃ, black.
ġaḃ, take.
liḃ, with you.
marḃ, dead.
raiḃ, was.
riḃ, you.
ſliaḃ, a mountain.
taoḃ, a side.
uġ, an egg.
aċt, but.

beaċ, a bee.
boċd, poor.
cloċ, a stone.
críoċ, the end.
cruaċ, a rick.
deiċ, ten.
deoċ, a drink.
drúċt, dew.
eaċ, a horse.
feuċ, behold.
fiaċ, a debt.
fliuċ, wet.
fuaċt, cold.

71. ġaċ, each.
loċ, a lake.
luċ, a mouse.
moċ, early.
naċ, not.
neaċ, any person.
noċ, who.
noċd, night, naked.
oċd, eight.
rioċd, shape.
ſeaċ, aside.
ſeaċt, seven.
ſġeaċ, a bush.

ſlioċd, progeny.
teaċ, a house.
teaċt, coming.
tráċd, converse.
uċt, the breast.
áḋ, good luck.
báḋ, love.
beiḋ, will be.
biaḋ, food.
bioḋ, let it be.
buaiḋ, victory.
buiḋe, yellow.
caoiḋ, lamentation.

72. criaḋ, clay.
croiḋe, a heart.
fáiḋ, a prophet.
réaḋ, extent.
fiaḋ, a deer.
feiḋm, use.
fleaḋ, a feast.
ġnoḋ, business.

ġnáḋ, love.
niḋ, a thing.
nuaḋ, new.
raḋ, a saying.
reiḋ, ready.
ruaḋ, red.
reaḋ, yes.
breáġ, fine.

bпıᵹ̇, virtue.
ѵeaᵹ̇, good.
ѵeoıᵹ̇, conclusion.
ѵıaıᵹ̇, end.
ѵoıᵹ̇, opinion.
laoᵹ̇, a calf.

leıᵹ̇, read.
lıaᵹ̇, a physician.
mıaᵹ̇, a field.
oᵹ̇, perfect, pure.
пıᵹ̇, a king.

---

73. ſleaᵹ̇, a spear.
ſluaᵹ̇, a troop.
ſuᵹ̇, juice.
ſuıᵹ̇, sit.
cıuᵹ̇, thick.
cпaıᵹ̇, strand.
cпuaᵹ̇, pity.
uaṁ, a cave.
aṁ, raw.
cnaıṁ, bone.
ѵaṁ, an ox.
ſпeaṁ, a root.
ᵹnıoṁ, an act.

laṁ, a hand.
naoṁ, a saint.
neaṁ, heaven.
neıṁ, poison.
пıaṁ, ever.
ſaṁ, pleasant.
ſᵹeıṁ, beauty.
ſnaṁ, swimming.
uaıṁ, a den.
aċ, a ford.
bıċ, existence.
blaċ, blossom.
bпaċ, judgment.

---

74. caıċ, chaff.
caċ, a battle.
cıoċ, a shower.
clıaċ, a hurdle.
cпıoċ, trembling.
cпuċ, form.
ѵaċ, colour.
ſeċ, a sinew.
ſuaċ, hatred.
ᵹuċ, voice.
ıċ, eat.
leaċ, half.
lıaċ, grey.
luaıċ, ashes.

maıċ, good.
meıċ, fat.
пıoċ, a race.
пoċ, a wheel.
ſaıċ, enough.
ſcıaċ, a wing.
ſᵹaċ, a shadow.
ſıoċ, peace.
ſnaıċ, a thread.
ſпuċ, a stream.
ceıċ, hot.
cпaċ, time.
cuaᵹ̇, a hatchet.
cuaċ, a country.

SECT. 3.—*Initial Aspirates.*

75. ѵo ḃaѵ, thy boat.
a ḃaſ, his death.

an ḃean, the woman.
mo ḃeul, my mouth.

a blar, his taste.

a blāċ, his blossom.

a bo, his cow.

mo bpac, my cloak.

mo bpón, my sorrow.

ɔo beiċ, to be.

mo ċac, my cat.

a ċeaɔ, his permission.

a ċeann, his head.

mo ċiop, my comb.

mo ċiop, my rent.

ɔo ċopp, thy body.

a ċop, his foot.

mo ċu, my hound.

mo ċuiɔ, my portion.

ɼa ċul, backwards.

a ɔaiɔ, his father.

o ɔeap, from the south.

mo ɔeoċ, my drink.

mo ɔeip, my right hand.

ɼa ɔo, twice.

mo ɔopnn, my fist.

mo ɔun, my fort.

po ɔub, very black.

---

76. ca ɼaɔ, how long.

an ɼail, the ring.

an ɼéil, the feast.

m' ɼeap, my husband.

a ɼip, O man.

po ɼliuċ, very wet.

a ɼolc, his hair.

po ɼuap, very cold.

an ɼuil, the blood.

po ʒann, very scarce.

mo ʒean, my love.

mo ʒiall, my jaw.

ɔo ʒlac, took.

ɔo ʒoiɔ, stole.

an ʒpian, the sun.

ɔo ʒab, seized.

an ʒaoċ, the wind.

ɔo ʒnaċ, usually.

mo ʒpaɔ, my love.

a ṁac, his son.

a ṁapc, his beef.

ca ṁéiɔ, how much.

mo ṁeup, my finger.

ɔo ṁian, thy desire.

a ṁic, O son.

ɔo ṁnaoi, to a woman.

po ṁop, very great.

a ṁuc, his pig.

---

77. po ṁaiċ, very well.

po ṁoċ, very early.

mo ṗáipc, my field.

mo ṗeann, my pen.

mo ṗian, my pain.

a ṗiob, his pipe.

an ṗluc, the cheek.

mo ṗóʒ, my kiss.

mo ṗopc, my tune.

ɔo ṗup, thy lip.

mo ṡál, my heel.

a ṡaoi, sir.

mo ṡiup, my sister.

ɔo ṡlac, thy rod.

o ṡoin, since.

ɔo ṡpón, thy nose.

mo ṡuil, my eye.

ɔo ṡuiɔ, sat.

ɔo ċip, thy country.

ɔo ċoʒ, took.

mo ċoil, my will.

ɔo ċuʒ, gave.

ɼa ċpi, thrice.

ɔo ċuic, fell.

D

o ċuṗ, from the beginning.
mo ċaoḃ, my side.

ṗo ċeiċ, very hot.
ṗo ċiuġ, too thick.

Sect. 4.—*Short Sentences with aspirated Monosyllables.*

78. ċa ṗe moċ.	It is early.
léiġ ḃam.	Let me alone.
bi ꝺo ċoṗc.	Be silent.
ca ṗaiḃ ꝼu?	Where have you been?
ma ċiġ leaꞇ.	If you can.
maiċ ꝫo leóṗ.	Very well.
ni ċiġ líom.	I cannot.
ꝼuiḃ ꝫo ꝼocaiṗ.	Sit still.
ꞇaiṗnꝫ an ċloꝫ.	Pull the bell.
bail o Ɗhia oṗꞇ.	God bless you.
ce ṗin aꝫ ꞇeaċꞇ?	Who is that coming?
ni'l a ꝼioṗ aꝫam.	I don't know.
ꝫo ꝺe a ċloꝫ e?	What o'clock is it?
bioḃ ṗe maṗ ṗin.	Let it be so.
ni'l ṗe ṗeiḃ ꝼóṗ.	He is not ready yet.
ca'ṗ ꝼaꝫ ꞇu e?	Where did you leave it?
ꝺ'uaiġ me mo ḃaoċain.	I ate enough.
cia aca ḃi ann?	Which of them was there?
cuiṗle mo ċṗoiḃe.	Vein of my heart.
ma 'ṗ é ꝺo ċoil e.	If you please.
iꝼ ꞇṗuaġ liom ṗin.	I am sorry for that.
na bioḃ eaꝫla oṗꞇ.	Do not fear.
ꞇa an leanḃ a ꝫul.	The child is crying.
iꝼ ꞇeiċ an aimṗiṗ ı.	It is warm weather.

---

79. ca ṁéiꝺ iꝼ ꝼiu iaꝺ?	How much are they worth?
an ṗaiḃ ꝼuaċꞇ oṗꞇ?	Were you cold?
ꞇa mo ṙaiċ aꝫam ꝺe.	I have enough of it.
ce'ṗ leiꝼ an ꞇiġ ṗin?	Whose house is that?

buo maiʈ liom a ƀeiɫ.	I would wish to be.
ruiƀ rior le mo ɫaoƀ.	Sit down by my side.
oo ƀi bean oear aiʒe.	He had a pretty wife.
beiƀ me leaʈ ʒo ʒoirio.	I will be with you soon.
ni reioir leo ʒan a ƀeiʈ.	They cannot but be.
naċ iorraiƀ ʈu nior mo ?	Will you not eat more ?
reuɫ an ʒrian aʒ oul raoi.	See the sun setting.
ni'l ʈu com aorʈaliomra.	You are not as old as I am.
ir raoa liom a o'ran ʈu.	I think you staid too long.
an ʈan oo ƀuail re e.	When he beat him.
ʈairbean ƀam an rʒian rin aʒao.	Shew me that knife you have.
oo ƀi a ʒruaʒ com ouƀ le ʒual.	Her hair was coal black.
ir mo an ʒraƀ ʈa aʒamra orʈ na ʈa aiʒeran.	I love you more than he.
ir mo ʒraƀ ʈa aʒam orʈra na airrean.	I love you more than him.
ʒo oe air a ƀruil riƀ a ʈráċo ?	What are you talking of?
ir e ro an rear a ċar orainn anoe.	This is the man that met us yesterday.

Sect. 5.—*Spelling Exercises.—Aspirated Dissyllables.*

80. aƀall, an apple.
aƀarc, a horn.
aƀmao, timber.
aʒmar, lucky.
amaɫ, out.
amáin, alone, only.
amainn, a river.
amrar, doubt.
amuiʒ, out.

anƀrann, feeble.
aoiƀinn, pleasant.
aoiƀnear, joy.
arƀar, corn.
earċu, an eel.
arʈeaċ, within.
aɫair, a father.
baoʒal, danger.
bacaɫ, lame, a cripple.

balaḋ, a smell.
bealaċ, a way.
beannaċo, blessing.
beaṫa, life.
blaṫaċ, buttermilk.
bliaḋain, a year.

boṫán, a hut.
bóṫaṗ, a road.
bṗaḋaċ, roguish.
bṗaᵹaḋ, the bosom.
bṗeiṫeaṁ, a judge.
bṗomaċ, a colt.

81. bṗónaċ, sorrowful.
bṗuiᵹṫe, boiled.
buaċail, a boy.
buiḋeaċ, thankful.
buailiḋ, a dairy.
buailṫean, a flail.
cailleaċ, a hag.
caoiṗḟeoil, mutton.
caṫaiṗ, a city.
ceaċṫaṗ, either.
cionṫaċ, guilty.
claiṗṗeaċ, a harp.
cliabán, a cradle.
cloiḋeaṁ, a sword.
· coiḋċe, always, ever.

coileaċ, a cock.
coiṁeaḋ, keep.
coṁṗaḋ, conversation.
coṗṁuil, like.
coṁṫṗom, just, equal.
cṗiaṫaṗ, a sieve
cṗuiṫneaċo, wheat.
cuiṁne, memory.
cumanᵹ, narrow.
cuṗṗṫa, weary.
cuṫaċ, furious.
oaoaḋ, a trifle, a jot.
oaiḋḃiṗ, poor.
oaṁṗa, dancing.
oanaċṫ, boldness.

82. oeaṫaċ, smoke.
oeiṁin, certain, true.
oeiṗḃṗiuṗ, a sister.
oeiṗeaḋ, end.
oioṁaoin, idle.
ooilᵹioṗ, affliction.
ooṁain, deep.
ooṁan, the world.
ooṁnaċ, Sunday.
oaoṫain, sufficiency.
ooṫċaṗ, hope.
oṗoiċioḋ, a bridge.
ouḃaiṗṫ, said.
éaḋaċ, clothes.
éaoṁaṗ, jealous.

eallaċ, cattle.
eaṗṗaċ, spring.
ein-neaċ, any one.
eiṗᵹe, rising.
eiṗiᵹ, arise!
eiṗoeaċṫ, audience.
eoċaiṗ, a key.
ḟaiṫċeaṗ, fear.
ḟaṗaċ, a desert.
ḟeaṗṫain, rain.
ḟiaḋain, wild.
ḟiṫċe, twenty.
ḟlaiṫeaṗ, heaven.
ḟoᵹlaim, learning.
ḟolaṁ, empty.

83. ᵹaḃa, a smith.
ᵹaḃaṗ, a goat.

zaoaióe, a thief.

zaóap, a hound.

zealac, the moon.

zeamap, grass-corn.

zeappiaó, a hare.

zeimpe, winter.

zopaó, heat, warming.

zpiopac, burning embers.

zuióe, a prayer.

iapacт, a loan.

inpip, marriageable.

inzean, a daughter.

iocoap, bottom.

ionznaó, wonder.

ionmuin, beloved.

ionmup, wealth.

laca, a duck.

leabap, a book.

leacan, broad.

leacap, leather.

leizean, a lesson.

leizeap, a cure.

leoman, a lion.

luaiтpeaó, ashes, dust.

luize, lying.

maoaó, a dog.

maizoean, a maiden.

mapac, morrow.

---

84. mapcac, a horseman.

mapzaó, a market.

mapтpeoil, beef.

maтaıp, a mother.

meaóon, the middle.

meamaip, memory.

meapbal, a mistake.

miтio, time.

moinpeup, a meadow.

mullac, a hill.

naoióin, an infant.

naomтa, holy.

neamzlan, unclean.

neapтmap, powerful.

neimzlic, unwise.

nuaióeacт, news.

ocpac, hungry.

ooan, a pan.

oióce, night.

oióeacт, lodging.

oiópe, an heir.

oiópeacт, an inheritance.

opuib, upon you.

papтap, paradise.

peacac, sinful.

peacaó, sin.

pinzin, a penny.

popaó, marriage.

ppéacan, a crow.

paóapc, sight.

---

85. paiтe, a quarter of a year.

peamap, fat.

piozacó, a kingdom.

paióbip, rich.

paozal, the world.

palac, dirty.

pampaó, summer.

rzópnac, the throat.

peacтmuin, a week.

peappac, a foal.

peancup, antiquity.

rzaтán, a mirror.

pioтcáin, peace.

pionnac, a fox.

pnaтao, a needle.

pneacтa, snow.

poizтeac, a vessel.

puaimneap, tranquillity.

D 2

ʀuιδe, sitting.
ᴄaɓaιn, give.
ᴄalaṁ, land.
ᴄapaιδ, quick.
ᴄeallaċ, a hearth.
ᴄιmċeal, about.
ᴄóιnneaċ, thunder.
ᴄonnaṁ, a wake.
ᴄoʀaċ, beginning.
ᴄʀaιċnín, a little straw.

ᴄʀoʀ5aδ, fasting.
ᴄuιnʀeaċ, tired.
uaċᴄaʀ, top, cream.
uaιne, green.
ualaċ, a burden.
uaċɓaʀ, wonder.
uιṁιʀ, number.
ullaṁ, ready.
uṁal, humble.
unnaι5e, prayer.

SECT. 6.—*Exercises in Reading.*

86. ιmċι5 ʀoṁaᴏ.   Go on.

laɓaιʀ amaċ.   Speak out.

nι ċuι5ιm ċu.   I do not understand you.

ʀeaċaιn ċu ʀeιn.   Mind yourself.

nι ʀuʀaʀ a ʀaδ.   It is not easy to say.

ʀa5 an bealaċ.   Leave the way.

5o maιʀeaδ ᴄu.   That you may live.

laʀ an ċoιnneal.   Light the candle.

cuιʀ aʀ an ċoιnneal.   Put out the candle.

ʀoʀ5aιl an ʀuιneó5.   Open the window.

ᴄaʀ a ʀιuɓal lιom.   Come walk with me.

nι ʀacaιδ me é.   I did not see him.

ca ʀaᴏa ʀaċaιδ ᴄu?   How far will you go?

an ʀaċaιδ mιʀe leaᴄ.   Shall I go with you?

na ᴄe amaċ 5o ʀoιll.   Do not go out for awhile.

nι δeaʀna me é.   I did not do it.

ᴄa ʀe a5 ʀeaʀċaιn.   It is raining.

ca h-uaιʀ a δ-ιmċι5 ʀe?   When did he go?

an laɓʀan ᴄu 5aoιδιl5?   Do you speak Irish?

ᴄeaδam 'n a ɓaιle.   Let us go home.

beιδ ʀeaʀċaιn a5uιnn.   We shall have rain.

ca ʀaιᴏe o ʀoʀaδ ι?   How long is it since she was married?

ᴄaɓaιʀ δam ᴏo laṁ.   Give me your hand.

87. níl amraŕ aiŕ bíċ aiŕ.   There is no doubt at all of it.

na leiᵹ óo imċeaċc.   Do not let him go.

níoŕ ċiᵹ leiŕ a faᵹail.   He could not get it.

abaiŕ leiŕ ceaċc aŕceaċ.   Tell him to come in.

cuiŕ an caiŕᵹíoo ċuᵹam.   Send me the money.

caiċfíó cu a beiċ coŕŕċa.   You must be tired.

ca m' aċaiŕ aᵹuŕ mo ṁaċaiŕ amuiᵹ.   My father and mother are out.

ca ŕí póŕca oŕ cíon coiċċíóiŕ   She is married over a fortnight.

ní ċiᵹ líom fuiŕeaċ níoŕ faíoe.   I cannot stop longer.

an é ŕo an bealaċ ᵹo Luimneaċ?   Is this the way to Limerick?

cía aca ŕo an boċaŕ ceaŕc?   Which of these is the right road?

an ŕuᵹ cu mo bŕoᵹa ċuᵹam?   Did you bring me my shoes?

a ca me foᵹlaim mo leiᵹínn.   I am learning my lesson.

88. na bí fanaċc feaó an lae.   Do not be staying all day.

ní ċŕeioim an ní a oeiŕ ŕe.   I do not believe what he says.

ca cu aᵹ ŕíubal ᵹo ŕo ᵹaŕoa.   You are walking too fast.

ca me oul a ċeannaċ líneaoaiᵹ.   I am going to buy linen.

bí ŕíao aᵹ ol oiᵹe aᵹuŕ aᵹ iċe bió.   They were eating and drinking.

ní ċiᵹ líom a labaiŕc ᵹo maiċ.   I cannot speak it well.

ταιm ρο búιδεαċ óυιτ α Shαoι.	I am very thankful to you, Sir.
nιᵹ̇ οο lαṁα αᵹυρ τ'αᵹαιὀ.	Wash your hands and face.
τα mo ὀαοċαιn ὀε αᵹαm.	I have enough of it.
ταρ αlειċ αᵹυρ οειn οο ᵹοραὀ.	Come here and warm yourself.
ὀ'ειριᵹ̇ me ᵹο moċ αιρ mαιοιn.	I rose early in the morning.
αρ ċοοαιl τυ ᵹο mαιċ α ρειρ.	Did you sleep well last night.
ταὀαιρ ιαραċτ οο ρᵹειne ὀαm.	Lend me your knife.
89. τα αn οοṁαn ᵹο lειρ αᵹ οul αnn.	All the world is going there.
ιρ mιċιο οuιnn οul ι leαbαιὀ.	It is time for us to go to bed.
α αnαm ρειn αιρ ᵹ̇υαlαnn ᵹαċ ειn-neαċ.	Every man's soul on his own shoulders.
buαιl mo ṁαορα, buαιl me ρειn.	Strike my dog, strike myself.
níl lειċ-ṗιnᵹ̇ιn αᵹαm óυιτ.	I have not a halfpenny for you.
ιρ mαιċ lιom ριn α ċlοιρτιnn.	I am glad to hear that.
ὀιomαρ αᵹ οul αρ αᵹαιὀ ᵹο ceαρτ ᵹο nuιᵹe ρο.	We were getting on well up to this time.
ιρ ιοmὀα ρεαρ ραιὀὀιρ ᵹαn ρuαιṁneαρ.	There is many a rich man without quiet.
ὀεαnρuιnn nιορ mo nα ριn αιρ οο ρonρα.	I would do more than that for your sake.
nι ρ̇αcα me í αċο αοn-υαιρ αṁαιn.	I never saw her but once.

naċaṗ aiṗiṗ me óuiᴄ ᵹan a ḃeiᴄ́ laḃaiṗᴄ coṁ aṗo ṗin ?	Did I not tell you not to be talking so loud ?
iṗ ᴄuṗa an leanḃ aḃ ionṁuine liom ṗa ᴄiᵹ.	You are the child I love best in the house.
ċainiᴄ ᴄu aṗᴄeaċ́ ṗaoi óeiṗeaḋ.	You came in at last.

---

90. Ḃhi áṗoċ́uṗ aiᵹe aiṗ na Scoᴄaiḃ i n-Eiṗinn aᵹuṗ i n-Alḃain.

He was sovereign of the Scots in Ireland and Albany.

Iṗ aiṗ éiᵹin ᴅo ċṗeioṗinn am inᴄinn ᵹo ṗaiḃ Eiṗe ṗiaṁ ṗa ċumaċᴄ na Roṁánaċ́.

I can scarcely be induced to believe that Ireland was at any time under the dominion of the Romans

A ᴄa a óeaṗḃ aca ṗein, aᵹuṗ aᵹ caċ́, ᵹuṗ aḃ clann ᴅ'Eiṗeannċaiḃ na Scuiᴄ.

It is a matter of certainty with themselves, and with every one, that the Scotch are descendants of the Irish.

Ꞇiᵹ Ḃeᴅa leiṗ an nió ṗo ṗan ċ́éaᴅ caiḃioil ᴅo'n leaḃaṗ ᴅo ṗᴄaiṗ Eaᵹlaiṗe na Sacṗan.

Bede agrees with this in the first chapter of the Book of the Church History of the English.

Ṗahe Colam Cille ceaᴅ Ꝺocᴄuiṗ an ċṗeiᴅiṁ Caᴄolice ᴅona Ṗicᴄi ṗan aiṗᴅᴄ́uaiċ́ aṗ na ṗleiḃᴄiḃ.

Columbkille was the first teacher of the Catholic faith to the Picts in the northern Highlands.

CHAPTER III.

ECLIPSIS.

SECT. 1.—*Of the Effects of Eclipsis in the Sounds of the Letters.*

91. ALL the mutable consonants, except m, are liable to lose their sound in certain cases where a letter is prefixed to them at the beginning of a word; in which cases the original initial is said to be *eclipsed* by that which is prefixed, and the sound of the latter only is in general heard in the pronunciation. The following list exhibits the different changes which are thus introduced in the spelling and sound of words:

b c o ꝼ p ꞃ ꞇ	is eclipsed by	m ᵹ n b b ꞇ o	as	aꞃ m-báo, our boat, aꞃ ᵹ-ciall, our reason, a n-ooiᵹ, their hope, a bꝼuil ꞇu, art thou, buꞃ b-páiꞃꞇ, your share, an ꞇ-ꞃlaꞇ, the rod, aiꞃ o-ꞇuꞃ, in the beginning,	pronounced	aꞃ máo. aꞃ ᵹial. a noiᵹ. a buil ꞇu. buꞃ báiꞃꞇ. an ꞇlaꞇ. laiꞃ ouꞃ.

ᵹ is but partly eclipsed by n, the sound of both letters uniting to form a compound, as *ng* in long, hang, &c., or as nᵹ in ainᵹeal; thus na n-ᵹoꞃꞇ, pronounced *nang urth, of the fields.*

92. The effect of eclipsis is sometimes expressed by doubling an initial letter instead of prefixing the letters above mentioned, as cc, ꝼꝼ, pp, ꞇꞇ, for ᵹc, bꝼ, bp, oꞇ, thus a cclan, *their children;* a ꝼꝼeaꞃan, *their land;* aꞃ ppáiꞃoe, *our*

child ; ɓuṗ ċċíṗ, *your country,* &c.; which are pronounced exactly as α ʒlαn, α ɓᵽeαṗαn, αṗ bαıṗoe, ɓuṗ oıṗ, &c.

93. In the middle of words ol and ln, both sounded like ll, thus, coolαó, *sleep,* and colnα, *of the flesh,* are pronounced collα; similarly on, as nn, so ceαonα, *the same,* sounds like ceαnnα.

SECT. 2.—*Short Sentences, with Eclipsis.*

94. αn ɓ-ᵽuıl ocṗαṗ oṗċ ?   Are you hungry ?

αn ɓ-ᵽuıl ṗe mαll ?   Is it late ?

cά ɓ-ᵽuαıṗ ċu é ?   Where did you find it ?

ċα ṗe ṗα n-ʒαıṗoın.   He is in the garden.

αn ɓ-ᵽuıl ċu ʒo mαıċ ?   Are you well ?

α ʒ-cluın ċu me ?   Do you hear me ?

ṗαınıc α n-ooıṗċᵽα é.   Take care lest you spill it ?

ċα beαn αʒ α n-ooṗαṗ.   There is a woman at the door.

αn ɓ-ᵽuıl ṗnαċαo αʒαo?   Have you a needle ? I have.
ċα.

nαċ o-ċuıʒeαn ċu me ?   Do you not understand me?

cά ɓ-ᵽuıl oo leαɓαṗ ?   Where is your book ?

αn ɓ-ᵽuıl ċu oά ṗıṗıɓ ?   Are you in earnest ?

cα o-ċeıo αn boċαṗṗα ?   Where does this road lead to?

αn ɓ-ᵽuıl αn oıneıṗ ullαṁ?   Is the dinner ready ?

95. αn ɓ-ᵽuıl ouıl αʒαo α óul ?   Do you wish to go ?

cα αṗ α o-ċαınıc ċu ?   From whence did you come ?

ċαṗ αṗċeαċ ṗα ċ-ṗeomṗα.   Come into the room.

αn o-ċuıʒeαn ċu ʒαoıó-ılʒ ?   Do you understand Irish ?

cα m-bıonn ċu oo ċoṁ-nuıʒe ?   Where do you live ?

ʒo m-beαnnuıʒe Oıα óıɓ.   God save you.

ιτ θοιξ ℓιοm ζο n-θεαnα τε ὲ.	I think he will do it.
ζο ξ-cuιτεαθ Οια αn τ-άξ οττ.	God prosper you.
τℓαn ℓεατ ζο ττειcιm ατιτ ὲυ.	Farewell till I see you again.
τιοcτα me α ξ-cεαn βεαζαnn ℓαετεαθ.	I will come in a few days.
cια αn τα β-τυιℓ τυ ταιτεαὲ?	Why are you alarmed?
ταβαιτ αιτε θυιτ τειn ζο θ-ταζα me.	Take care of yourself until I come.
cια αn uαιτ α θ-τιοcτα τυ αnτο αιτ?	When will you come here again?
ζο θε mατ α n-ζοιτεαn τυ το?	What do you call this?
nιℓ τε τα m-βαιℓε α θυιnε ὲοιτ.	He is not at home, good man.

---

96. θο τεατ ι n-α τιαθnuιτε τάοιτεαὲ θ'uαιτℓιβ α ὲτιὲε ζο τℓαιτ n-θι-τιξ mβάιn ι n-α ℓάιm.

There stood in his presence a chief of the gentlemen of his country, with a straight white wand in his hand.

τάnζαθατ ζαn αmτυτ αn ιοmαθ ό'n Spάιnn ό'n β-Ϝταιnc αζυτ ο'n m-Ϭτεαταιn αnn το.

There came hither very many, no doubt, from Spain, from France, and from Britain.

Sεαὲτ mbℓιαζnα θέαζ αζυτ cειὲτε τιὲιθ αιτ τεαὲτ ccέθ ι nθιαιθ nα θιℓεάn θο βαὲαθ Ϸhατατ.

Seven hundred and ninety-seven years after the flood Pharaoh was drowned.

Iſ coſmuıl bſeaċ naıġ
aʒuſ Ʒaoıbıl ı n-a
noſaıb aʒuſ ı n-a
m-béaſaıb ſe ċeıle.

The Welsh and the Irish are like one another in their customs and in their manners.

---

97. A ᴐeıſ Caımbſenſıſ
ʒuſ ab ſe lınn Neıll
Naoíʒıalluıʒ ᴐo beıċ
ı bſlaıċeaſ Eıſeann
ᴐo ċuaᴐaſ ſeıſeaſ
mac Muıſeaᴐaıʒ, ſıʒ
Ulaᴐ, ʒo h-Albaın.

Cambrensis mentions that it was in the time when Niall of the Nine Hostages was ruler of Ireland, that the six sons of Muireadhach, King of Ulster, went over to Scotland.

A ᴐeıſ ſé ſoſ ʒuſ ab
ſá 'n am ſın ᴄuʒaᴐ
Scoᴄıa ᴐ'aınm aıſ
Albaın aıſ ᴄᴄuſ,
aʒuſ ʒuſ ab ó'n
ʒ-ᴄloınn ſın ſıʒ Ulaᴐ
ʒaıſmᴄeaſ cıneaᴐ
Scuıᴄ ᴐ'Albanċaıb.

He says further, that it was at that time the name of Scotland was given to Albany, and that it was from those sons of the King of Ulster that the Albanians are called the Scottish race.

Ʒhabaᴐaſ luċᴄ na Scı-
ᴄıa aſoſlaıċeaſ ʒo
ʒſoᴐ ı n-ᴐıaıᴐ na ᴐı-
lıonn.

The people of Scythia attained supremacy shortly after the deluge.

---

98. Ꝺo bı ſoʒluım, aʒuſ
cſeᴐıoṁ, aʒuſ ſeaċᴄ,
aſ coıṁeaᴐ a n-Eı-
ſınn(ᴐo ſeıſ Keating),
aſ ſeaᴐ ceıᴄſe ċéaᴐ

Learning, and faith, and justice flourished in Ireland (according to Keating) for the space of four hundred years, after the

E

bliaḃain o'éiṛ Paṫṫ-
ṗuic oo ṫeaċṫ, ɀo
ṫeaċṫ Loċlonnaċ ınn-
ṫe.

arrival of Patrick, even to
the coming of the Danes.

Aṛ m-beiṫ ooPhaṫṛuiɀ
aɀ ṛíolaḋ an ċṛeıoıṁ
ın-Eıṛınn ı ḃ-ḟlaiṫioṛ
Laoɀaıṛe, aṛ é Aon-
ɀuṛ mac Naṫḟṛaoiċ
ṛa Rıoɀ Muṁan.

When Patrick was propaga-
ting the faith in Ireland,
in the reign of Laoghaire,
Ængus mac Natfraic was
King of Munster.

A oeıṛ cuıo oo na ṛean-
uɀoaṛaıḃ ɀuṛ ab a
n-Ɀleann oa loċa a
n-ıaċṫaṛ Laıɀean ṛu-
aıṛ Naoṁ Paṫṫṛuic
baṛ; bıoḋ ɀo n-ab-
ṛuıo oṛonɀ oıle ɀuṛ
ab an Aṛomaċa oo
éaɀ ṛe.

Some of the old authors
state, that it was in Glendalough, in the lower part
of Leinster, that Saint
Patrick died; although
others assert that it was
in Armagh he departed
this life.

---

99. Iṛ a ḃ-ḟlaiṫioṛ Ḋoṁ-
naıll ṛóṛ ṛuaıṛ an
naomh Fıonnṫan o'á
n-ɀoıṛṫı Munna báṛ.

It was moreover in the reign
of Domhnall that Saint
Fintan, who is named
Munna, died.

Aṛ ṫṛe ɀuıḋe coṁṫion-
oıl Chıaṛaın a ɀ-Clu-
aın mıc Noıṛ, ṛuɀ
Ḋıaṛmuıo, macAoḋa
Slaıne, buaıḋ ċaṫa
Caıṛn Chonnuıll.

It was through the prayer
of the congregation of
Kieran of Clonmacnoise,
that Dermod, son of Aodh
Slaine, obtained the vic-
tory in the battle of Carn-
connell.

Oċṫ m-bliaḋna aɀuṛ
ceiṫṛe ṛıċṫ ṛa h-aoıṛ

The age of Brian Boru, when
he fell in the battle of

oo ōhnian ōonoiṁe Clontarf, was eighty-eight
an ṫan oo ċuiṫ ı years.
ʒ-caṫ Chluana ṫanb.

Sect. 3.—*Reading Lessons.*

[From Keating's History of Ireland.]

100. Ṁan bıon fón cıon aʒ
an n-Єineannaċ an
na neanċaoaıb, an an
n-aon oána, aın na
bánoaıb, aʒun an aon
neanma na ʒ-claın-
neaċ, b'oō a ṁaṁaıl
nın oo cıon aʒ an
m-ōneaċnaċ an an
on.oınʒ ʒ-céona, aʒun
bıo ṁan nın conṁaıl
ne céıle ı monán oo
béanaıb eıle.

As the Irishman also has a
love for the antiquaries,
the poets, the bards, and
the harpers, the Welch-
man has a similar regard
for the same people ; and
they resemble each other
in like manner in many
other usages.

I n-aımnın fón an céao
hennı ı níoʒaċṫ Shac-
ran, oo bı nnıonnna
an an m-ōneaṫaın
oan b'aınm Ǒnıfın áp
Conan, oo ṁaoıōeaō
ʒo mınıc ʒun bean
Єineannaċ fa máṫaın
ōo féın, aʒun fón fa
nean-ṁaṫaın, aʒun
ʒun ab ı n-Єinınn oo
nuʒaō aʒun oo béan-
ṁunaō é.

In the time likewise when
Henry I. was King of
England, there was a
prince in Britain named
Griffin ap Conan, who fre-
quently boasted that his
own mother was an Irish-
woman, and his grand-
mother likewise; and that
he himself was born and
educated in Ireland.

101. I g-ceann fealad aimsire do ġlac an Bhreatain i n-diaiḋ na m-Breaṫnaċ agus na b-Pict, an treas ċineaḋ i g-cuid no i mír na b-Pict, cineaḋ do ṫriall a h-Eirinn mar aon re n-a d-taoiseaċ Reuda, do ġreamuiġ i mearc na b-Pict ionad suiḋe dóiḃ féin, le cairdeas no le h-airm a tá i n-a seilḃ gus an am so.

After some interval of time, there took possession of Britain, besides the Britons and the Picts, a third race, in the portion or district of the Picts, a race that emigrated from Ireland, together with their leader Reuda, who seized upon a place of settlement for themselves among the Picts, by friendship or by arms, which is in their possession to the present time.

As so is follus gur ab a h-Eirinn do ċuadar cineaḋ Scuit le Reuda a d-taoiseaċ féin go h-Albain, agus go ḃ-fuilid a slioċt ann ó ṡoin, agus gur ab díoḃ gairmṫear Scuit.

From this it is evident that it was from Ireland that the Scottish race came, with their general Reuda, to Scotland; and that their posterity are there since that time, and that it is from them the Scots are so called.

Gibé leiġfeas Eoin Baronius 'san leaḃar do sgrioḃ do ḃesaiḃ agus do nósaiḃ an uile ċineaḋ, do ġeaḃaiḋ go follus ann naċ ionann nóis ná béasa

Whoever will read John Baronius, in the book that he wrote concerning the manners and customs of all nations, will there find clearly, that the customs and manners of the French

na b-Ƒɼancaċ aȝuɼ
na n-Eɼeannaċ anoɼ
ná a naḻóᴅ.

and of the Irish are not
the same now, and that
they have not been so in
time past.

---

102. Iɼ móɪᴅe ɪɼ ɪnċɼeɪoċe
ȝaċ níᴅ ᴅa n-ᴅubɼa-
maɼ ᴅo leɪċ ċaɪoɼɪṁ
na m-óɼeaċnaċ leɪɼ
na h-Eɼeanncaɪb,
aȝuɼ ȝuɼ b'í Eɼe ɼá
ċúl ᴅíoɪn ᴅóɪb, maɼ
a ᴅeɼ Caɼaᴅocuɼ
uȝᴅaɼ óɼeaċhnaċ ɪ
n-a ċɼoɪnɪc, aȝuɼ
Ɑbɪan, aȝuɼ ɪomaᴅ
ᴅ'uȝᴅaɼuɪb eɪle na
m-óɼeaċnaċ, ȝo ᴅ-cɪȝ-
ᴅíɼ móɼán ᴅo ɼɼɪonn-
ɼaᴅuɪb na m-óɼeaċan
aȝuɼ ᴅ'á n-uaɪɼlɪb
ȝo n'a muɪɼeaɼ aȝuɼ
ȝo n-a muɪnnċɼ ɪ
n-Eɼɪnn, maɼ a nȝab-
ċaoɪ ɼɪu, aȝuɼ maɼ a
n-ȝlacċaoɪ ȝo cɪnéal-
ᴛa ɪaᴅ, aȝuɼ maɼ a
ᴅ-ᴛuȝċaoɪ ɼeaɼann ɼe
a áɪᴛɪuȝaᴅ, aṁaɪl a
ᴅubɼamaɼ ċuaɼ. Ɒo
ȝní ɼoɼ Ɒocᴛoɼ Han-
mer ɪ n-a ċɼoɪnɪc
ɼɼeɼɪalᴛaċċ aɼ ċuɪᴅ

All that we have said about
the acquaintance of the
Britons with the Irish,
and with regard to the
circumstance that Ireland
was their last place of refuge, is the more credible,
inasmuch as Caradocus, a
British author, states in
his Chronicle (as well as
Abian, and several other
of the British authors),
that many of the princes
of Britain, and of their
nobles, used to come, with
their followers and people,
to Ireland, where they
were received and treated
with kindness, and were
given land to dwell on, as
we said above. Moreover,
Dr. Hanmer, in his Chro-
nicle, makes particular
mention of some of them.
First, he says, that there
was banished to Ireland
by Edwin, son of Ethel-
fred, a king that reigned

 oíob. Ꞇp o-ꞇúp a ꝺeıp ꝣup oíbpeaꝺ ꝣo h-Ꝺıpınn le Ꝺaꝺbuın, mac Ꝺeꞇelꝼpeꝺ, pıꝣ ꝺo bı ap an m-ꝺpeaꞇaın ꝺap b' aınm Caꝺbaıllın, an ꞇan ꝼa haoıp ꝺo'n Ꞇıꝣeapna pé céaꝺ aꝣup cúıꝣ ꝺéaꝣ ap ꝼíceaꝺ blıaꝺna, aꝣup ꝣo b-ꝼuaıp ꝣabáıl pıp ꝣo ꝣpáꝺaé ann, aꝣup ꝼuaıp conꝣnaṁ pluaıꝣ lép bean pe a ꝼlaıꞇeap péın amaé apíp. Ꝺ ꝺeıp póp ꝣo ꝺ-ꞇánꝣaꝺap ꝺá ꝑpıonnpa ó ꝺhpeaꞇaın, map a ꞇa Ꝺpolꝺ aꝣup Conan, ꝣo h-Ꝺıpınn, an ꞇan ꝼa h-aoıp ꝺo'n Ꞇıꝣeapna míle aꝣup ꝺeıé 'p ꝺa ꝼíceaꝺ blıaꝺna, aꝣup ꝣo b-ꝼuaıpeaꝺap a n-ꝣlacaꝺ, aꝣup póp caıꝺpeaṁ aꝣup cuṁꝺaé ó Ꝺıpeanncuıb.

in Britain whose name was Cadwallin, in the year of our Lord 635, and that he was there kindly received, and obtained an auxiliary force of troops by which he regained his own sovereignty again. He also says, that there came from Britain two princes named Harold and Conan, in the year of our Lord 1050, and that they met with a kind reception, and further, friendship and protection from the Irish people.

103. Iap m-baꞇaꝺ luéꞇa na h-Ꝺꝣıpꞇe 'pan Muıp Ruaıꝺ, an ꝺpꝺnꝣ ꝺo'n ꞇıp ꝺo ṁaıp ꝺ'á n-ꝺéıp

When the Egyptians were drowned in the Red Sea, the people of the country who lived after them ba-

oo puaʒɼao ouɪne
uaɼal o'aɪɼɪ́ɉɕe Sceɪ-
ɕɪaѣaɕ oo ѣíɪ n-aɕoṁ-
nuɪѣe eaɕoɼɼa, ʒo
naɕ n-ʒeaѣaѣ ꝼlaɪ-
ɕeaɼ oɼ a ʒ-ceann.
Cɼ m-beɪɕ oó aɼ n-a
ѣíbɪɼɕ ʒo n-a ɕɼeɪѣ,
ɕaɪnɪc ʒuɼ an Spaɪnn,
maɼ aɼ áɪɕɪɉ ɼé
ɪomao blɪaona aʒuɼ
a n-oeaɕaoaɼ a ɼlɪoɕɕ
ɪ líonṁaɪɼeaɕɕ ʒo
móɼ, aʒuɼ ɕanʒaoaɼ
aɼ ɼɪn ɪ n-Єɪɼɪnn.

Cɼ oeɪɼɪo cuɪo oo na
nuaѣ-Ժhalluɪѣ ɼɪ, aʒ
ɼcɼíoѣaѣ aɼ Єɪɼɪnn,
ʒuɼ ab ó'n m-Ѣɼea-
ɕaɪn móɼ ɕánʒaoaɼ
mɪc Mɪleaѣ aɪɼ o-ɕúɼ,
aʒuɼ ɪɼé ɼáɕ ɼá ɼaoɪ-
lɪo ɼɪn, oo ѣɼɪʒ ʒo
ѣ-ꝼuɪlɪo ɪomao ꝼocal
ɪonannɪ ɪ m-Ѣɼeaɕnaɪɼ
aʒuɼ ɪ n-Ժaoɪѣeɪlʒ.

nished a certain Scythian
chieftain that was living
among them, that he
might not assume sove-
reignty over them. Hav-
ing been banished with
his tribe, he came to
Spain, where he lived
many years, and where
his posterity became very
numerous ; and from that
they came to Ireland.

Some of the modern English,
writing about Ireland, as
sert that it was from
Great Britain the sons of
Milesius came originally,
and their reason for think-
ing so is, that there are
several words the same in
the British and in the
Irish.

---

104. Nɪ ɪonʒnaѣ ɪomao ꝼo-
cal oo ѣeɪɕ ɪonann
ɼan Ѣhɼeaɕnaɪɼ aʒuɼ
'ɼan Ժhaoɪѣeɪlʒ, ʒɪon
ʒuɼ ab o'n m-Ѣɼea-
ɕaɪn ɕánʒaoaɼ mɪc

It is no wonder that there
are many words the same
in Welsh and in Irish,
although it was not from
Britain the sons of Mile-
sius came into Ireland :

Mileaḋ i n-Eirinn, ᴅo bríġ ġur bí Eipe ra cúl víoin ᴅo ḋḣreaċnaіḃ pe linn ġaċ leaċtpom ᴅá luiᴅeaḋ oppa ᴅo ċoіrc na Roṁánaċ no na Saġpanaċ, no ġaċ ᴅpoinġe eile ᴅa n-impeaḋ roipneapt oppa, ionnur ġo ᴅ-tiġᴅír roipne iomᴅa ġo n-a muipeap aġup ġo n-a muinntip ap teiċeaḋ i n-Eirinn ᴅioḃ, ġo ᴅ-tuġᴅír uairle na h-Eireann reapann ap reaḋ a ġ-cuapta ᴅóіḃ, aġup an rlioċt ᴅo ċiġeaḋ uaċa pe linn a n-ᴅeopuiġeaċta ᴅo roġlamċaoi an Ġhaoiᴅeilġ leo, aġur atáiᴅ bailte i n-Eipinn ainmniġteap uaċa, map a taᴅpaiġ na m-ḋreaċnaċ, aġup Ðún na m-ḋreaċnaċ, 7c. Aġur iap ᴅ-tilleaḋ ᴅo'n ḋreatain ᴅóіḃ, ᴅo bíoᴅ iomaᴅ rocal ᴅo 'n Ġaoiᴅeilġ ap ġnáċuġaᴅ aca

because Ireland was the last refuge of the Britons in the time of every trouble that befel them from the invasion of the Romans or Saxons, or any other people that visited them with oppression. So that there came many of the inhabitants of Britain, with their families and retainers, fleeing into Ireland, where the nobles of Ireland gave them land during their stay; and the Irish was learned by their children who were born during the time of their sojourn; and there are towns in Ireland that are named after them, such as Graigue-na-Mana and Dunmanway, &c. And after their return to Britain, there were many Irish words in common use among themselves, and their posterity after them. According to what we have said, it is not necessary to suppose that the sons of Milesius came originally from Britain, al-

αξυρ αξ α ρlιοċċ ο'α n-éιρ. Do ρéιρ α n-ουϧραμαρ nι h-ιn-ṁεαρτα ξο h-éιξεαn-ταċ, ξυρ αϧ o'n m-ϧρεαταιn τάnξα-ϧαρ mιc Mιlεαϧ αιρ ϧ-τύρ, ταρ ċεαnn ξο ϧ-ϝυιlιϧ ϝοcαιl ιon-αnn ι m-ϧρεαċnαιρ αξυρ ι n-Ϧαοιϧειlξ.

Α ϧειρ Séαραρ, ραn ρειρεαϧ lεαϧαρ ο'α ρταιρ, ξυρ αϧ ó οι-léαnυιϧ nα ϧρεαταn ϧο ċυαιϧ ϧραοιτε ϧο'n Ϝhραιnc. Ιρ ιnṁεαρ-τα ξυρ ϧ'é οιléάn nα h-Ειρεαnn αn τ-οι-léάn ριn αρ αρ ċρια-lαϧαρ nα ϧραοιτε, ϧο ϧριξ ξυρ ϧ'í Ειρε το-ϧαρ ϧραοιϧεαċτα ιαρ-ċαιρ Εορρα αn ταn ριn, αξυρ ξυρ ϧι αn Ϧαοιϧεαlξ ϝα τεαnξα ϧο nα ϧραοιċιϧ ċéαϧ-nα.

though there be some words identical in the Welsh and Irish lan-guages.

Cæsar says, in the Sixth Book of his History, that it was from the British Isles the Druids came to France. It is probable that the Isle of Erin was that island from which the Druids emigrated, be-cause Ireland was the source of the Druidic sys-tem of the west of Europe at that time, and Irish was the language of the Druids.

CHAPTER IV.

READING LESSONS (RELIGIOUS AND MORAL).

SECT. 1.—*From Gallagher's Irish Sermons (with the Orthography corrected).*

105. Ɔ'ιαρρ ριαɔ τρόϲαιρε αɴ υαιρ α ɓι ρι ρε ραȝαιl αϲα, αȝυρ ɔα ɓριȝ ριɴ ρυαραɔαρ í.

They asked for mercy when it was within their reach, and therefore they obtained it.

Ɑɴ μαιοιɴ, αɴ υαιρ ρορȝlυρ ρυιɴɴεοȝα αɴ lαε, ιρ ϲóιρ ɓúιɴɴ ρυιɴɴεοȝα αρ ɴ-αɴμα ɔ'ρορȝυιlτ, ρο ϲόṁαιρ ȝραρα αɴ Ⱡιȝεαρɴα, αȝυρ α ɴ-ορυιο α ɴ-υȝαιɓ ȝαϲ ɔροϲ ρυιɴ αȝυρ ȝαϲ ϲαϲυȝαιɓ.

In the morning, when the windows of day open, we ought to open the windows of our souls to the grace of the Lord, and shut them against every evil thought and temptation.

Ɑρ ɴιɓ ȝɴάϲ ɔο'ɴ μαϲτιρε αɴυαιρ α ϲέιο ρε ρο αɴ τρέαɔ, ɓρειϲ αρ ρϲορɴαιȝ αρ αɴ ȝ-ϲαορα αȝυρ αɴ τεαɴȝα α ȝεαρραɓ αιρϲε ȝαɴ ṁοιll, αρ ϲειρϲε ȝο ɴ-ɔεαɴαɓ ρí μέιlεαϲ ɴο τορραɴ, ṁυρϲοlαɓ αɴ τρευɔαιɓε, ɓέαρραɓ ϲοɓαιρ ɓι.

It is a usual thing with the wolf, when he goes into the flock, to seize a sheep by the throat, and cut its tongue out directly, for fear lest it should raise a bleating, or noise, that might awaken the shepherd to come to its aid.

Caṿ aṟ ṟo ṽ-ṫuᵹann ṫú ṫaṗcuiṟne no mioṁoṽ ṽo'n ṟeaṗ úṽ eile, ṫá boċṫ no uiṗiṟioll, aᵹuṟ ᵹuṗ ionann aṽ-maṽ ṽ'a n-ṽeaṗnaṽ ṟiḃ, maṗ aṫa an lu-aṫṟeán.

What is the reason that you shew contempt or uncivility to that other person that is poor or humble, while the material of which you are both made is one and the same, namely, ashes.

---

106. Má ṫá ṟéiṗion a ṟṫaiṽ na n-ᵹṟaṡ, aᵹuṟ ṫuṟa a b-peacaṽ, iṟ ṟeáṗṗ eiṗion míle uaiṗ no ċuṟa, cuiṗ a ᵹ-cáṟ ᵹo ḃ-ṟuil ṫú aṽ' ṟiᵹ no aṽ' Phṗionnṟa. Aċṫ an maiċ leaṫ ṟᵹeula ṽ'ṟaᵹail, a ċṗioṟṽaiᵹe, caṽ ṟo m-bíonn na ṽaoine aṗ laṟaṽ ṗe ṗún ṽioᵹal-ṫuiṗ? Caṽ aṟ a m-bío aṗ meiṗᵹe ṗe ᵹṟaṽ an ṫ-ṟaiṽḃṗiṗ? Caṽ aṟ a m-bío ṫuc-ċa ṽo ċṟaoṟ, aᵹuṗ ṽo ᵹaċ ainṁian? Caṽ aṟ a m-bío ṫucċa ṽo ṁionna móṗa, ṽo ᵹa-ṽaiṽeaċṫ, aᵹuṗ ṽo ḃṟeaᵹaiḃ? Aṫá 'ṽeiṗ an Ṟaiṽ Ṟiᵹeaṁail, ṽo ḃṟiᵹ ᵹo n-ṽéiniṽ ṽeaṗmaṽ ṽo'n ḃáṟ.

If he be in a state of grace, and you in sin, he is a thousand times better than you, although you be a king or a prince.

But, Christian, would you learn why it is that men are inflamed with the secret passion of revenge? Why they are intoxicated with the love of riches? Why they are given to excess and to every lust? Why they are given to swearing? It is, says the Royal Prophet, because they forget death. (Ps. lxxiii.)

Caᴅ aꞃ naċ ꞃinuaineann τú, a ꞃeaċuiᵹ, ᵹo m-beiċ an cholainn ꞃin, ꝼo ɓ-ꝼuil τú anoiꞃ aᵹ ᴅéanaṁ a n-iomaᴅ cúꞃaim, 'na biaᴅ piaꞃτ aᵹuꞃ cnuoᵹ, ꝼaoi ċeann ᵹeáꞃꞃ aimꞃiꞃe.

Why is it, sinner, that you do not reflect, that that body, on which you now spend so much care, shall in a short time be the food of worms.

---

107. Aτá ꝼóꞃ ᴅa niᴅ cꞃuτuiᵹioꞃ ꞃiaċτanuꞃ ꞁa h-uꞃnaiᵹe, maꞃ aτá, móꞃᴅaċτ aᵹuꞃ maiτeaꞃ Ꝺé ᴅo τaoɓ, aᵹuꞃ boċτaineaċτ aᵹuꞃ eaꞃɓuiᴅ an ᴅuine ᴅo'n τaoɓ eile.

Ꝺhéaꞃꝼa ꞃe óiɓ ᵹaċ niᴅ biaꞃ ꞃiaċτanaċ aᵹaiɓ annꞃa τ-ꞃaoᵹal ꞃo, aᵹuꞃ an ᵹlóiꞃ ꞃioꞃꞃuiᴅe annꞃa τ-ꞃaoᵹal eile.

Aτa ᴅaille na n-ᴅaoineaᴅ ċoṁ móꞃ aᵹuꞃ ꞃin, ᵹo ꞁ-ᵹlacaiᴅ an uile cúꞃam ꝼo neiτiɓ ᴅiombuan an τ-ꞃaoᵹail ꞃo, aᵹuꞃ ᵹo n-ᴅéanaiᴅ neaṁɓꞃiᵹ ᴅo ꝼaiᴅɓꞃeaꞃ ꞃioꞃꞃuiᴅe Phaꞃꞃτaiꞃ.

There are, moreover, two causes that give rise to the necessity of prayer, namely, the majesty and goodness of God on the one side, and the poverty and want of man on the other side.

He will give you every thing that shall be needful for you in this world, and in the other world, life eternal.

The blindness of mankind is so great, that they take all care of the transitory things of this world, and treat as worthless the everlasting blessings of Paradise.

ʒé naċ b-ꝓuil níó aꞃ biċ
annꞃa' τ-ꞃaoʒal ꞃo iꞃ
coiτċinne iná an báꞃ,
oo bꞃiʒ ʒo ꞃúblann
ʒo laeċaṁail eao-
ꞃainn ó ċiʒ ʒo τiʒ, ʒo
b-ꝓuaoáiʒionn ꞃiꞃ an
τ-óʒ maꞃ an áꞃꞃuió,
aʒuꞃ ʒo o-τaiꞃnʒeann
iao ċum na h-uaiʒe,
an uaiꞃ iꞃ luʒa oo
ꞃaoilio; maiꞃeaó, 'na
óiaió ꞃo aʒuꞃ uile, ní
ꝓuil níó aꞃ biċ iꞃ
euꞃʒaióe o'á n-oéan-
τaꞃ oeaꞃmao, iná oo'n
m-báꞃ.

Although there be nothing
in this world that is more
common than death, be-
cause it stalks daily
among us from house
to house, sweeps away
young as well as old, and
draws them into its pit,
at the time when they
least think of it; notwith-
standing, after all this,
there is nothing in the
world more readily for-
gotten than death.

---

108. Iꞃ ionʒanτuꞃ móꞃ ꞃo
ʒan aṁꞃuꞃ, aʒuꞃ ʒan
níó aꞃ biċ aꞃ an
τ-ꞃaoʒala ꞃ a n-oeaꞃ-
camaoio naċ ʒ-cuiꞃ-
eann an báꞃ a
n-aoṁail óúinn. Má
óeaꞃcamaoio ꝓúinn aꞃ
an τalṁain oéaꞃꞃaió
an τalaṁ linn, naċ
b-ꝓuil ionainn, aċτ cꞃé
aʒuꞃ luaiτꞃeán. Má
ꝓéaċamaoio ꞃuaꞃ aꞃ
an aeꞃ, oeaꞃbaió an
τ-aeꞃ óúinn, nac

This is much to be won-
dered at, no doubt, since
there is nothing in the
world upon which we
lay our eyes, that does
not bring death before
our notice. If we look
beneath us on the earth,
the earth will say to us,
that there is nothing in
our composition but
earth and ashes. If we
look up towards the air,
the air will indicate to
us that there is no con-

F

ḃ-ꝼúıl ꝺo ḃuaıneaꞃ ı
n-áꞃ m-beaṫa, aċꞇ
uꞃaꝺ le ꞃéıꝺeán
ᵹaoıṫe. Má ꝺeaꞃ-
camaoıꝺ uaınn aꞃ an
ḃ-ꝼaıꞃᵹe, aᵹuꞃ aꞃ na
ꞃꞃoṫannaıḃ, cuıꞃꝼıꝺ
a n-úṁaıl ꝺúınn ᵹo
n-ımṫıᵹeann áꞃ n-aım-
ꞃıꞃ aᵹuꞃ áꞃ ꞃaoᵹal
ṫoꞃaınn ᵹan ṁoṫuᵹaꝺ,
aꞃ aıꞃꞇe an ꞇ-ꞃꞃoṫa.

I n-aon ꝼocal, ní ꝼuıl
ꞇaoḃ ꝺ'á ꝺ-ꞇıonꞇoċa-
maoıꝺ naċ ḃ-ꝼuıl
ıoṁáıᵹ an ḃáıꞃ oꞃ aꞃ
ᵹ-coṁaıꞃ; máıꞃeaꝺ
a n-aıṁꝺeoın ᵹaċ
oıꝺeaꞃa aᵹuꞃ ᵹaċ
ꞃaḃa ꝺíoḃ ꞃo, a ꞇá
ꝺaılle na n-ꝺaoıneaꝺ
ċoṁ móꞃ aᵹuꞃ ꞃın, naċ
ḃ-ꝼuıl níꝺ aꞃ bıṫ ıꞃ
luaıṫe ꝺa n-ꝺéanaıꝺ
ꝺeaꞃmaꝺ no ꝺo'n
m-báꞃ.

109. An uaıꞃ a ċꞃuṫuıᵹ Oıa
áꞃ ꞃınnꞃıꞃ Aꝺaṁ aᵹuꞃ
Eaḃa, ꞃınne ꞃe maıᵹıꞃ-
ꞇıꞃ ꝺíoḃ aꞃ ᵹaċ aoıḃ-
neaꞃ, aᵹuꞃ aıꞃ ᵹaċ
ꞇoꞃꞃṫa ḃí a b-Paꞃꞃ-
ṫaꞃ, aċꞇ cꞃann na

tinuance in our life, but
what a breath of wind
possesses. If we look
away from us on the sea,
and on the streams, they
will put us in mind that
our time and our age is
going by imperceptibly,
like the flowing of the
stream.

In a word, there is no side
to which we can turn,
where the image of death
does not meet us ; yet,
in spite of every lesson
and every warning, such
as these, the blindness of
men is so great that
there is nothing at all
more speedily forgotten
by them than death.

When God created our
forefathers, Adam and
Eve, he put them in
possession of evey en-
joyment and every fruit
which was in Paradise,
but the tree of knowledge

h-Qiéne amáin. Qɼuɲ
ıonnuɲnaċ m-bɲıɲɲıóíɲ
an Qıéne ćuıɲ ɲo oɲéa,
'ɲé ɲın, ɼan blaɲ oo
éoɲéa an éɲaınn ɲo,
ćuıɲ an báɲ oɲ a
ɼ-comaıɲ, maɲ ɲcıaé-
óíoın, aɼuɲ maɲ óaın-
ɼean a n-aɼaıó ɼaé
caéuɼaıó. Qéé maɲ oo
ćonnaıɲc an Oıabal,
ɼo o-cıubɲaó cuımne
an báıɲ oɲéa beıé
úmal oo Ohıa, aɼuɲ
ɼan an aıéne ɲo oo
bɲıɲeaó, óıbıɲ ɼan
moıll an oeaɼɲmuaın-
eaó ɲo aɲ a ɼ-cɲoıó-
éıb, aɼ oeaɲbuɼaó
óóıb, naé ɲaıb baoɼal
aɲ bıé báıɲ oɲéa, cuıɲ
a ɼ-cáɲ ɼo n-íoɲɲaıóíɲ
an é-uball ɲo, oo bí
cɲoɲéa oɲéa. Qéé cao
é o'eıɲıɼ o'áɲ ɲınnɲıɲ
aɲ an cɲeaɲon aɼuɲ
an eaɲumlaéé ɲo
ɲınneaoaɲ a n-aɼaıó
ólıɼe Oé? Qéá a
Chɲıoɲoaıóe ɼuɲ ćaıll-
eaoaɲ aıbío na n-ɼɲáɲ
a ćuıɲ Oıa ɲo n-a
n-anam. Chaılleaoaɲ

only. And that they
might not break this
commandment which He
enjoined upon them, that
is, that they should not
taste the fruit of this
tree, he set before them
death as a preservative
and fence against every
temptation. But when
the devil saw that the
remembrance of death
would cause them to be
obedient to God, and not
to break this command-
ment, he banished, with-
out delay, this good
thought from their
hearts, certifying to
them, that there was no
danger of death happen-
ing to them, supposing
they should eat this apple
that was prohibited to
them. But what happen-
ed to our first parents in
consequence of their trea-
son and the disobedience
with which they treated
the law of God? It was,
Christian, that they lost
the habit of grace with
which God endued their

scéiṁ neaṁḋa, do cruṫuiġeaḋ leo; an t-anam a ḃí 'n a ṗéarla uasal lonnraċ, do réir ioṁaiġe agus ċosaṁlaċta Dé, gur ṫiontoiḋ an peacaḋ í, ċum a ḃeiṫ duḃ, smearṫa, glonnṁar, do réir ioṁáiġe agus cosaṁlaċta an diaḃail. O'n a m-beiṫ 'n a maiġistriḃ ar an b-Parrṫas talṁaiḋ so, agus 'na n-oiġriḋiḃ ar Pharrṫas neiṁe, díbreaḋ iad lomnoċtuiḋ gan earraḋ, gan eadaċ, ar feaḋ an t-saoġail; agus ċailleadar a g-ceart ar ḟlaiṫeaṁnus. A n-áit a ḃeiṫ saor ar an m-bás, agus ar gaċ tinneas ar feaḋ a d-tearma ar an t-saoġal so; mar ḃárr pionnuis ar a n-easumlaċt, ṫáinic tinneas agus aicíḋíḋe orrṫa féin, agus ar a slioċt 'n a n-diaiḋ: agus da ḋruim sin an bás.

soul. They lost the heavenly beauty that was created with them; the soul, that was a noble shining pearl, after the image and likeness of God, sin changed, so that it should be dark, defiled, loathsome, after the image and likeness of the devil. From being the owners of this earthly paradise, and heirs of the paradise of heaven, they were driven out naked, without goods, without clothing, through the wide world; and lost their right to heaven. Instead of being free from death, and from every disease, during their stay in this world; as a punishment imposed for their disobedience, there came sickness and disease upon them, and upon their posterity after them, and besides this, death.

110. Iʃ uime cʃuċuiᵹ Ɔia an ꝺuine ċum ᵹo m-beiċ ʃé ꝓann-ꝓáiʃꞇeaċ annʃa'nᵹlóiʃ ʃioꝓʃuiꝺe, aᵹuʃ 'n-oiᵹʃe aʃ ꝓhaꝓꝓċaʃ. Cċ ꞇaʃ éiʃ an ċine ꝺaonna ꝺo cailleaṁain a ᵹ-ceaʃꞇ ċum na h-oiᵹʃeaċꞇa ʃo, ꞇʃé ꝑeaċaꝺ Cꝺaiṁ; ꞇaʃ éiʃ iaꝺ ꝺo beiꞇ 'n a náṁꝋiꞃ aᵹ Ɔia le mílꞇiꞃ bliaꝺan aᵹuʃ 'na ʃcláꞃuiꝋċiꞃ aᵹ an ꝺiaꞃal; ᵹeaꞇuiꝺe Phaꝓꝓċaiʃ ꝺo beiꞇ ꝺúnꞇa 'na n-aᵹaiꝺ aᵹuʃ iʃʃionn ꝺo beiꞇ béal-ꝑoʃcailꞇe ʃo n-a ᵹ-coṁaiʃ; an ʃaoᵹal a beiꞇ aᵹ ꞇʃeuᵹꞃail an Ɔé ꝑíʃ, a cʃuċuiᵹ iaꝺ, aᵹuʃ aᵹ ꝺeanaṁ aꝺʃaiꝺ aᵹuʃ iobaiʃꞇe ꝺo na ꝺéiċiꞃ bʃéiᵹe; ċúiʃlinᵹ ꝑo ꝺeiʃeaꝺ mac Ɔé aʃ na ꝑlaiċiʃ; ᵹlac colann ꝺaonna a m-bʃoinn na Ⅿaiᵹꝺine Ⅿuiʃe. Caʃ éiʃ e beiꞇ ꞇʃi bliaꝺna ꝺéaᵹ aʃ ꝑiċio aʃ an ꞇ-ʃaoᵹal ʃo a m-boċꞇaineaċꞇ,

It was for this end God created man, that he be a partaker of everlasting glory. But after mankind having lost their rights to this inheritance through the sin of Adam; after their being enemies to God and slaves of the devil for thousands of years; the gates of Paradise shut against them, and hell opening its mouth before them; the world gone astray from the true God, that created them, and offering adoration and sacrifice to false gods: at last the Son of God came down from heaven and assumed human flesh in the womb of the Virgin Mary. After he had been thirty-three years in this world in poverty and sorrow, undergoing distress and hardships, while he taught and instructed the people by words and by example, he suffered at length the shameful death of the

aʒuⲣ a n-anⲣó, ⲅaoı
ḃuaⱱaıⲧ aʒuⲣ ⲅaoı
ⲉ́ⲣıoblóıⱱ aʒ ⲣⱬıⲣⲣaⱱ
aʒuⲣ aʒ ⲧeaʒaⲣʒ na
poıbleaⲥ́ ⲣe bⲣıaⲥ́naıḃ
aʒuⲣ ⲣe ⲣompla, ⱱ’ⲅu-
laınʒ ⲅo ⱱeⲙeaⱱ́ báⲣ
ⲣcannalaⲥ́ na ⲥⲣoıⲥ́e ;
ⱱ’oⲅⲣaıl ⲣe é ⲣéıⲛ maⲣ
ıoⱱ́baıⲧ ⱱoⲛn Cⲧ́aıⲣ
ⲣíoⲣⲣuıⱱe, ıonnuⲣ ʒo
n-ⱱéanⲅaⱱ́ ⲣé aⲣ ⲣíoⲥ̇-
ⲥ́áın ⲣıⲣ; ⲣıⲣ b-ⲅuıʒeaⱱ́
aⲣ aıⲣ an bⲣⲉıⲥ́ ⱱa-
manⲧa ⲧuʒaⱱ́ ’n áⲣ
n-aʒ́aıⱱ́ a b-ⲣⲉaⲣⲣaın
Cⱱaıⲙ̇.

If you say, Christian, that
God shewed mercy to
the thief on his right
hand in the point of
death, after his having
been before in wicked-
ness; and that it *may be*
he will shew the like
mercy to you. Alas,
poor sinner, you have
nothing for that but
" may be ;" and if you
risk eternity on a " may
be," you give the world
to understand, that you

---

cross; he offered himself
as a sacrifice to the eternal Father, to make our
peace with him, and
reverse the judgment
of condemnation passed
against us in the person
of Adam.

111. Ⲙa ⱱeıⲣ ⲧú, a Cⲏⲣıoⲣ-
ⱱaıⱱe, ʒo n-ⱱéaⲣna
Ⲇıa ⲧⲣócaıⲣe aⲣ ʒ́a-
ⱱaıⱱe na láıⲙe ⱱeıⲣe
a b-ⲣonⲧ, aⲣ báıⲣ,
ⲧaⲣ éıⲣ a bⲉıⲥ́ ⲣıaⲙ
ⲣe h-olⲥ; aʒuⲣ ʒo
mb’ⲅéıoıⲣ ʒⲉ n-ⱱéan-
ⲅaⱱ́ an ⲧⲣócaıⲣe
ⲥéaⱱna oⲣⲧ-ⲣa. Oⲥ̇, a
ⲣeacuıʒ́ ḃoıⲥ́ⲧ, ní ⲅuıl
aʒaⱱ aıⲣ ⲣın, aⲥⲧ
b’ⲅéıoıⲣ, aʒuⲣ má
ⲥuıⲣeann ⲧú an ⲧ-ⲣíoⲣ-
uıⱱeaⲥⲧ a ʒ-conⲧaḃ-

αιρτ ρe b'ғéιοιρ, ḃeιn τu le τuιȝριn oo 'n τ-ραοȝαl, naċ ḃ-ғuιl meaρ aȝαo aρ an nȝlóιρ ҏιορρuιȯe, naċ ḃ-ғuιl beann aȝαo aρ oo ҏlanuȝαȯ ná acaρa aρ bιċ ρe ριαnταιḃ Iғғριnn. Ƒuαιρ an ȝαoαιȯe ρo, ȯeιn Ναoṁ Cluȝuιρτιn, τρócαιρe a b-ponc an ḃáιρ, ταρ éιρ a ḃeιċ ριαṁ 'na ҏeαcαċ, ιonnαρ naċ m-beιċ euoóċċuρ αρ αon n-ȯuιne. Clċτ ó ċúρ an τ-ραοȝαιl ȝo o-τí an uαιρ ρo, ní léιȝτeαρ αιρ αon n-ȯuιne, ċuιρ an αιċ-ριȝe ȝo ponc an ḃáιρ, ғuαιρ τροcαιρe, αċτ an τ-αon ȝαouιȯe ρo, αȝuρ mαρ ριn ní ғuιl áȯḃαρ anoóċċuιρ αȝ αon n-ȯuιne.

have no regard for eternal glory, that you have no respect for your salvation, nor any concern about the pains of hell. This thief found mercy at the point of death, says St. Augustine, after having been always a sinner, that none might despair. But from the beginning of the world to this present hour, there is none read of that put off repentance to the point of death, who found mercy, but this one thief, and so no person has a cause for presumption.

---

112. Ҭhuȝ Ðια annρ α' τ-ρeιnρeαċτ αιċne αȝuρ oρouȝαȯ oo 'n ċιne oαona ȝρáȯ oo ḃeιċ αca aρ an ȝ-co-

God in the old law gave to mankind a commandment and injunction to love their neighbours. The Jews, through ig-

ṁapṟainn. Oo ṁeaṟ
na luoaıże ṫṗé aın-
bṟıoṗ, naċaṗ oṗouıż-
eaò an aıċne ṟo óóıḃ
aċṫ żṗáò a ḃeıċ aca
aṗ a ż-cáıṗoe, ażuṗ
żuṗ ḃ-ṟéıoıṗ oóıḃ ṟuaċ
a ḃeıċ aca aṗ a náıṁ-
oıḃ. Aċṫ ıonnuṗ żo
n-oéanṟaò loṗa Cṗíoṗṫ
eoluṗ óóıḃ a n-áıṫ an
aınḃṟıṗ ṟo, ażuṗ ṗoluṗ
na n-żṗáṗ a n-áıṫ an
ooṗċaoaıṗ ı n-a ṗaḃa-
oaṗ, laḃṗaıò żo ṗoıléıṗ
a   n-oıuṁ   ṗıṗ   an
ṫ-ṗaożal. Ḃheıṗ oṗ-
oużaò   żeneaṗalṫa
óoıḃ, naċ leóṗ oóıḃ
żṗáò a ḃeıċ aca aṗ a
ż-cáıṗoe, aċṫ ṟóṗ żuṗ
eıżın oóıḃ żṗáò a ḃeıċ
aca aṗ a náıṁoıḃ,
maıċ a òéanaṁ a
n-ażaıò an uılc, ażuṗ
a ḃeıċ·aż żuıòe aṗ ṗon
na muınṫıṗe ıṗ mo żní
oíożḃáıl oóıḃ.

norance, imagined that
this commandment did
not order them to love
any but their friends,
and that they might en-
tertain hatred towards
their enemies. But to
the end that Jesus Christ
might communicate to
them knowledge instead
of this ignorance, and
the light of grace instead
of the darkness in which
they were involved, he
now speaks plainly to the
world. He gives them
a general order, that it
is not enough for them
to love their friends, but
that they must also love
their enemies, do good
in return for evil, and
pray for the people that
do them most injury.

---

113. Oéaṗṟaıò ṗíḃ lıom, żan
aṁṗaṗ, żuṗ níò ooıò-
éanṫa żṗaò a ḃeıċ

You will tell me, no doubt,
that it is a hard thing
for us to love the person

αʒαιnn αp αn τé, ɔ'á
ɓ-ꝼuιlmιɔ cιnnτe ꝼuaτ
α ɓeιτ αιʒe oppαιnn;
ʒpáɔ α ɓeιτ αʒαιnn
αp αn τé, ɓeιp míoclú
αʒuꝼ ꝼcαnnαl ɔúιnn;
αʒuꝼ nατ ꝼτopαnn o
αon níɔ, ɔéαnꝼαɔ
ɔíoʒɓáιl no ɔoluιʒ
ɔúιnn; αττ ɔeιpιmꝼe
lιɓ-ꝼe, ɔ'á cpuαταnαιɔ
ɔα ɓ-ꝼuιl ꝼé, ʒuꝼ αb
óιʒιn α ɔéαnαm; ɔo
ɓpιʒ, ʒo ɓ-ꝼuιl Cpιoꝛτ
ɔ'α ópouʒαɔ óιɓ: αʒuꝼ
nατ ɓ-ꝼuιl cuꝼ ꝼuαꝼ
αʒαιɓ ʒαn α τoιl ɔo
ɔéαnαm.

who, we are certain,
cherishes hatred towards
us; to love the person
that makes use of re-
proach and reviling to-
wards us; and who will
not stop at any thing that
may cause us damage or
loss: but I tell you, that
however hard it be, it
must be done, because it
is Christ that bids you
do it, and that you can-
not resist doing his will.

---

114. Má ɔeαꝛcαmαoιɔ αꝼ
αn náɔúιꝼ ιnnτe ꝼéιn,
ɔo ɓpιʒ ʒo ɓ-ꝼuιl níoꝼ
mó ɔo claon αιce cum
αn uιlc, no cum nα
mαιτeαꝼα, ιꝼ nιɔ ɔoιɔ-
éαnτα ꝼo αιce. Cττ
má ɔeαꝛcαmαoιɔ uιꝼꝼ-
τe ꝼαoι ꝼτιuꝼαɔ nα
n-ʒꝼáꝼ, αn níɔ ꝼo α τá
ɔóιɔéαnτα αιce, ʒeιɓιɔ
ꝼí é ꝼoιɔéαnτα ꝼocαm-

If we look to nature in it-
self, because it is more
inclined to evil than to
good, this is a hard thing
for it. But if we look
upon it under the gui-
dance of grace, the thing
that is difficult for it, it
will find easy and prac-
ticable. Christ enjoins
upon us nothing that is
hard. He puts upon us

laċ. Ní oꞃouiȝeann
Cꞃíoꞃᴄ nío aꞃ biċ
ꝺóiꝺéanᴄa ꝺúinn. Ní
ċuiꞃeann ualaċ oꞃainn
naċ ꝺ-ᴄiȝ linn a ioṁ-
ċaꞃ.

no burden that is impos-
sible for us to bear.

---

115. Ní fuil ꝺuine aꞃ biċ
ꝺeaꞃcaꞃ aꞃ na h-áꝺ-
ꞃaꞃaiꝺ ȝluaiꞃeuꞃ é
ċum ȝꞃáꝺ ꞃeiċ aiȝe aꞃ
a náiṁoiꝺ, naċ ȝ-cuiꞃ-
fíꝺ cꞃuaᴄan aiꞃ féin,
aꞃ ꝺóiȝ a ꝺeanᴄa. Cn
ċeaꝺ áꝺꞃaꞃ ꝺíoꝺ; ȝuꞃ
óꞃꝺaiȝ Cꞃíoꞃᴄ ꝺúinn a
ꝺéanaṁ, aȝuꞃ ꝺá ꞃꞃiȝ
ꞃin, ȝo ꞃ-fuil ꝺ'fiaċ-
aiꝺ oꞃainn a ċoil ꝺo
ꝺéanaṁ. Cn ꝺaꞃa
h-áꝺꞃaꞃ, ȝuꞃ ȝꞃáꝺuiȝ
Cꞃíoꞃᴄ féin a náiṁꝺe
aꞃ an ᴄ-ꞃaoȝal ꞃo,
aȝuꞃ ȝo ꞃ-fuil ꝺ'fiaċ-
aiꝺ oꞃainne aiċꞃiꞃ ꝺo
ꝺéanaṁ aiꞃ. Cn ᴄꞃeaꞃ
áꝺꞃaꞃ, an ᴄé naċ
ꝺ-ᴄuȝann maiċeaṁnaꞃ
ꝺ'á náiṁoiꝺ, ní ꞃ-fui-
ȝíꝺ ꞃé maiċeaṁnáꞃ.

There is no person who
considers the causes that
bind him to love his
enemies, that will not
force himself to do it.
The *first* of these causes
is, that Christ has en-
joined us to do it, and
that for this reason we
are bound to do what
is his will. The *second*
cause is, that Christ
himself loved his enemies
in this world, and that
we are bound to imitate
him. The *third* cause is,
that he who forgives not
his enemies, shall not
obtain forgiveness him-
self.

---

116. Féaċ anoiꞃ, a Cꞃꞃíoꞃ-
ꝺaiꝺe, an connꞃaꝺ aᴄá

Behold now, Christian, the
covenant that exists be-

eıoıp Oıα αᵹυρ αn ουıne. Ɱά ḋαıċeαnn ċú, mαıċρıὁeαρ ὁuıċ. Ɑᵹυρ cuıρeαnn ċu-ρα ρeαlα αρ αn ᵹ-connραὁ ρo, ċoṁ mınıc αᵹυρ α ὁeıρ ċú ὁo Ρhαıoıp, ċoṁ mınıc αᵹυρ α ὁeıρ ċu, mαıċ ὁúınn άρ ɓ-ρı- αċα ὁo ρéıρ mαρ ṁαıċımío ᵹαċ ρıαċα, αᵹυρ ᵹαċ cuıρċe ᵹníċ- eαρ 'n άρ n-αᵹαıὁ; mά ɓρıρeαnn ċu-ρα αn connραὁ ρo, mά ɓıonn ċú ὁαnαρρċα, cρuαὁα- lαċ, neαṁċρócαıρeαċ ρe ὁo ċoṁαρραın, beıὁ Oıα ὁıɓeıρᵹeαċ, ὁıo- ᵹαɓċαc, neαṁċρócαı- ρeαċ, leαċ.

tween God and man. If you forgive, you shall be forgiven. And to this you set your seal as of- ten as you say the Lord's prayer ; as often as you say, *forgive us our debts, as we forgive every debt and every offence that is done against us ;* if you break this covenant, if you be harsh, cruel, unmerciful to your neighbours, God will be unforgiving, ruthless, and unmerciful to you.

---

117. Ƞαċ ɓ-ραıcımío ᵹo lαe- ċαṁαıl luċċ nα mıonn móρ, ċoṁ leαᵹċα ċum α ṗeαcαὁ ρo ċαρ éıρ ραoıρıo'n, αᵹυρ ὁo ɓíoὁαρ α ρıαṁ ρoıṁe ? Ƞαċ ɓ-ραıcımío luċċ nα ὁρúıρe, ċoṁ clαon ċum α' ṗeαcαὁ ρo α n-ὁıαıὁ ραoıρıoın, αᵹυρ ὁo ɓíoὁαρ α ρıαṁ

Do we not see daily, those who are ın the habit of swearing, as much given to this sin after confes- sion of it as they were before ? Do we not see the profligate as much inclined to their sin after confession, as they ever were before ? Do we not see the dishonest

poiṁe? Naċ ḃ-ɼaıcı-
mío luċc na ṁeallcó-
ɼaċca, aȝuɼ na ȝaṅaıȝ-
eaċca, coıṁ leaȝċa
cuṁ cuıṅ na ȝ-coṁaɼ-
ɼan cap éıɼ ɼaṫıɼıoın,
aȝuɼ ṅo ḃíoṅaɼ, a ɼıaṁ
ɼoıṁe? Caṅ é ıɼ cıall
ṅo ɼo, a ċáıɼṅe? O !
acá eaɼḃaṅ ṅóláıɼ ṅo
ḃeıċ oɼɼċa ó ċɼoıṅe.
Ṅa m-beıċ ɼuaċ ṅíɼeaċ
aca aɼ an ḃ-ɼeacaṅ,
ṅo ɼeıɼ maɼ oɼṅuıȝeaɼ
an aıċɼıȝe ɼıɼınneaċ,
níoɼ ḃ-eaȝal ṅóıḃ cuı-
cım ann coṁ luaċ ɼo.

and thievish as much
given to pilfering their
neighbours' goods after
confession as they ever
were before it. And
what is the meaning of
all this, my friends ?
Alas ! it is that they are
without contrition of
heart. Had they con-
ceived a just hatred of
sin, such as true repen-
tance implies, there
would have been no fear
of their falling so soon
as this.

Sect. 2.—*Extracts from Richardson's Irish Sermons (with the Orthography corrected).*

118. Iɼ mınıc ḃıoɼ an cuıṅ
ıɼ meaɼa aȝ an oɼuınȝ
ıɼ ɼeaɼɼ, aȝuɼ an cuıṅ
ıɼ ɼeaɼɼ aȝ an oɼuınȝ
ıɼ meaɼa, muɼ aınm-
nıȝeaɼ luċc an c-ɼaoȝ-
aıl ɼo ıaṅ. Aċc an lá
ṅéıȝıonaċ cıompoċaɼ
an cáɼṅa; oıɼ ann ɼın
béıṅ ȝaċ uıle ṅɼoċ ní
ṅ'áɼ ɼéıoıɼ a ɼmuaı-
neaṅ aȝ luċc na n-olc

Oftentimes the best men
have the worst, and the
worst the best things, as
they are called, of this
world. But at the last
day the scene shall be
quite changed : for then
all that were ill men
shall have all the ill
things that can be ima-
gined, and nothing at all
that is good, as we have

αᵹυη ní ḃeιὸ αon ní
maιċ αca: αn ταn
ḃeιὸ ᵹαċ ní maιċ ὀά
ḃ-ηέαοαιο ο'íαηηυιὸ,
αᵹ na οαoιnιḃ maιċe,
αᵹυη ᵹαn οηοċ ní αη
bιċ αca: muη ὀeαηḃαη
άη ο-τιᵹeαηna ὀúιnn,
αᵹ ηαὸ, ηαċηαιο na
ηίηέιn ċum na beαċα
ηιοηηυιὀe. αᵹυη ιη
ιαο ο'ά n-ᵹoιηċeαη
ηίηέιn αnn ηo maη ċuᵹ
me οom αιηe ċeαnna
o na ηαnnαιḃ oιle οe'n
ċαιbιoιl ηe, αn luċτ
α ċηeιοιοη α n-Ιοηα
Cηíoητ, αᵹυη υιme ηιn
οά ο-τυᵹαnn ηέ cu-
ṁαċτα ċum ηιυḃαιl α
n-αιċeαnταιḃ, αᵹυη α
n-όηουιᵹċιḃ αn Cι-
ᵹeαηna ᵹαn ṁιlleάn,
maη οo ηιnneαοαη
Sacάιηιαη αᵹυη Elιη-
ebeᴢh, αᵹυη αη αn
άὸḃαηηιn α οeιηċeαη
ᵹo ηαḃαοαη αηαon ηί-
ηέαnτα α ḃ-ηíαὸnαιηe
Οέ.—Ⱡu. ι. 6.

already seen ; whereas, all who were good men, shall have all the good things they can desire, and nothing at all that is bad, as our Lord here assures us, by saying, "the righteous shall go into life eternal." Where, by the righteous, as I have already observed in general from the context, we are to understand such as believe in Jesus Christ, and therefore are enabled by him to walk in all the commandments and ordinances of the Lord blameless, as Zacharias and Elizabeth did, and that reason are both said to be "righteous before God."—Lu. i. 6.

---

119. αn ουιne ηαιὸḃιη úὸ, οo ḃí α n-έαοαċ coη-

That rich person that "was clothed in purple and

cpa, aᴣup lín mín,
aᴣup ap na biaċaċ ᴣo
po-póᴣaṁuil ᴣaċ aon
lá, an uaip ʋo ċuaiċ
pé ᴣo h-ıᵱepn, ní paıḃ
aon ḃpaon aṁáın uıp-
ᴣe aıᴣe ná uıpıoʋ ap
a leanᵱaċ hápp meoıp
ʋuıne ʋo ċomᵱaċ ann.
Ꝿuc, xvi. 19, 24.

fine linen, and fared
sumptuously every day;"
when was got to hell,
he had not " one drop of
water," not so much as
would stick " to the tip
of a man's finger," when
dipped into it.—Luke,
xvi. 19, 24.

---

120. Aᴣup an ċé ʋ'á ʋ-ċuᴣ
a ċalaṁ ċopaċ coṁ
h-ıomaʋaṁuil pın, naċ
paıḃ pmuaıneaċ aıᴣe
ap aon ní, aċċ a pᴣıo-
bóıl ʋo léıᴣeaċ píop,
aᴣup a n-ʋeanaṁ níop
ᵱaıppınᴣe, ċum ᴣo
m-bíaċ áıċ aıᴣe ı n-a
ʋ-ċaıpċeoċaċ a ıolṁaı-
ċeap; ıp· beaᴣ ʋo ᵱaoıl
pé ᴣo pᴣappaċ pıu ᴣo
bpáċ. Aċċ caʋ ʋu-
baıpċ ᵱpeaᴣpaċ Ꝺé
pıp ? A amaʋáın,
anoċċ ᵱéın ıappᵱuı-
ċeap h'anam opċ, ann
pın cıa aᴣa m-beıċ na
neıċe ʋo ᵱoláıp ċu ?
Ꝿu. xvii. 20. Cıa aᴣa
m-beıċ ? Ní aıᴣe-
pean ᴣan aṁpap. Ꝺo
b'éıoıp ᴣo m-beıċʋíp

And he whose ground
brought forth plenti-
fully, so that he thought
of nothing but pulling
down his barns and
building greater, that he
might have where to
treasure up his goods;
he little thought of ever
parting with them. But
what said the answer of
God to him ? " Thou
fool, this night shall thy
soul be required of thee;"
then whose shall these
things be which thou
hast provided ? Whose
shall they be ? None of
his be sure. Other peo-
ple, perhaps, may enjoy
them for awhile, as he
did ; but he, for his
part, will have no share

ṗeal aᵹ oaoiṁḃ oile
maṗ ḃáoaṗ aiᵹeṗean;
aċt aṗ a ṗon ṗan, ni
ḃeiṗ ċuio aṗ bioċ aiᵹe
ṗioḃ; ní ḃeiṗ aiᵹe aon
ṫṗoiᵹ oo'n ṫalṁain,
ná aon ṗpṗúille oo'n
aṗán, aon ḃṗaoin oo'n
uiṗᵹe, aon ċeiṗṫ oo'n
éaoaċ, ná aon ṗeoiṗ-
linᵹ o' aiṗᵹioo lé n-a
ᵹ-ceannaċ, oa ḃ-ṗaᵹaḃ
le n-a ᵹ-ceannaċ iao.
Oo imċiᵹ uaiḃ anoiṗ
an ṁéio oo ṗaoṫṗuiᵹ
ṗe aṗ ṗeaḃ a ṗaoᵹail,
ᵹan aṗ a ċumaṗ a
o-ṫaḃaiṗṫ aṗ a n-aiṗ
ᵹo bṗáċ. Oo b'éioiṗ ᵹo
ṗaiḃ ṫeaᵹ bṗeaᵹ ṗeal
aiᵹe, aᵹuṗ an iomao
o'eaṗṗaḃ ṗaioḃiṗ ann;
aċt anoiṗ ní ṗuil áiṫ
a ᵹ-cuiṗṗeaḃ a ċeann
aiᵹe, aċt a meaḃon
laṗṗaċ aᵹuṗ ṫeinṫeaḃ.
Oo ḃí ṗeaṗuinn, no
mainéiṗ, aᵹuṗ oo b'ṗei-
oiṗ iomao piᵹeaċṫa ᵹo
h-iomlán ṗeal i n-a
ṗeilḃ; aċt a noiṗ iṗ
mó ṫá aᵹ ṗeaṗ íaṗṫa
na oéiṗce iṗ boiċṫe aṗ
an ṫalṁain iná aiᵹe-

at all in them, not so
much as one foot of land,
one crumb of bread, one
drop of water, one rag
of clothes, nor so much
as one farthing of money
wherewith to buy it if
he could. All that he
laboured for all his life
long, it is now all gone,
past all possibility of
being ever retrieved. He
had once, perhaps, a fine
house to live in, with a
great deal of rich furni-
ture; but now he hath
not where to lay his
head, but in the midst
of flames of fire. He
had once farms, or ma-
nors, and, perhaps, se-
veral whole kingdoms,
in his possession; but
now the poorest beggar
upon earth hath more
than he. He once had
a great many friends;
but now he hath not
one in all the world.
He used to have gold
and silver, and a great
many fine things, as he
thought; but now he
lives in the very extre-

ɼeαn; ꝺo bí uιṁιɼ ṁóɼ
ꝺo cáιɼꝺe ɼeαl αιȝe;
αcꞇ αnoιɼ nι ꝼuιl αon
cαɼαιꝺ 'ɼαn ꞇ-ɼαoȝαl
uιle αιȝe: bá ȝnáꞇ leιɼ
αιɼȝeαꝺ, αȝuɼ óɼ ꝺo
beιꞇ αιȝe, αȝuɼ ιoмαꝺ
ꝺo neιꞇιb bɼeáȝα, мαɼ
ṁeαɼ ɼéιɼeαn ιαꝺ; α
ꞇá ɼé αnoιɼ α n-ꝺαoɼ-
bɼuιꝺ nα bocꞇαιneαɼα,
α n-ꝺíꞇ ȝαc uιle neιꞇe
ꝺo ꝺeαnαꝺ мαιꞇ óó, no
ꝺo ṁeαɼαꝺ ɼé ꝺo óeαn-
ɼαꝺ ɼoȝnαṁ óo.

mity of penury, in the
want of every thing that
can do him any good, or
that he could imagine
would do so.

121. Ꞇαιɼbeαnꞇαɼ nα neιꞇe
ɼo uιle ȝo ɼo-ȝlαn lé
ceαꝺ bɼιαꞇɼαιb nα bɼe-
ιꞇe, cαnnuɼ αn bɼeι-
ꞇeαṁ α n-αȝαιꝺ óɼu-
ιnȝe nα láιṁe clí, eα-
óon, ιмꞇíȝíó uáιm-ɼe;
óιɼ ó cαιꞇꝼιo ιмꞇeαcó
uαιó-ɼeαn αn αon-
ṁαιꞇ, ιɼ éιȝιn ꝺáιb ιм-
ꞇeαcꞇ ó ȝαc uιle ṁαιꞇ
αɼ ṁoó nαc m-beιó
ɼιoɼ мαιꞇeαɼα αcα ȝo
bɼáꞇ αɼιɼ. Ꭺȝuɼ o
ꝺeιɼ ɼe, α lucꞇ nα мαl-
lαcꞇ ȝo ꞇeιne ɼíoɼ-
ɼuιóe, uιme ɼιn béιꝺ

All this is plainly signified
by the first words of the
sentence which the judge
shall pronounce against
those on left hand :—
" Depart from me ;" for
in that they must de-
part from him, the only
good, they must needs
depart from all manner
of good, so as never to
know what it is any
more. And he adds,
" ye cursed, into ever-
lasting fire ;" they will
be thereby condemned
also to all manner of

ᴅαmαnᴄα ċum ᵹαċ
uɪle ꝓoꝗᴄ uɪlc, ɪꝗ ꝓéɪ-
ᴅɪꝗ leo ċuɪᵹꝗɪn no ṁo-
ċúᵹαᴅ. Cᵹuꝗ ɪꝗ leɪꝗ
ꝗo ᴅo ꝓáɪöᴄeαꝗ peαn-
nαɪᴅ nα ᵹ-céαᴅꝓα : αꝗ
αn αöbαꝗ, nαċ b-ꝓuɪl
αon ċeuᴅꝗα α ꝗᴄɪᵹ
nα αmuɪᵹ αcα ɪ n-α
ᵹ-coꝗꝗ, nα ɪ n-α n-αn-
mαnnαɪb nαċ m-beɪö
ᴅ'á b-ꝓɪαnαö ꝓɪꝗ αn
b-peαnαɪᴅ ꝗo, mαꝗ ċuɪ-
ꝗeαꝗ αꝗ ᴅ-ᴄɪᵹeαꝗnα
ꝓéɪn α ᵹ-céɪll öuɪnn,
αn ᴄαn αɪᴄnɪᵹeαꝗ öuɪnn,
eαᵹlα beɪċ αᵹuɪb ꝓoɪṁ
αn ᴄe leꝗ ꝓéɪᴅɪꝗ αn
ᴄ-αnαm αᵹuꝗ αn coꝗꝗ
ᴅo ꝗᵹꝗɪoꝗ α n-ɪꝓeꝗn.
Mαċ. x. 28.

evil, which they can any
way perceive or feel.
This is called the punishment of sense, because
all their senses, both in-
ward and outward, both
soul and body, shall be
affected with it ; as our
Lord himself also inti-
mated, where he re-
quires us to fear him
who is able to destroy
both soul and body in
hell. Math. x. 28.

---

122. Sᵹꝗɪoꝗꝓuɪöċeαꝗ ɪαᴅ α-
ꝗαon αn ꝗɪn, αn ᴄ-α-
nαm, αᵹuꝗ αn coꝗꝗ:
ní öéαnꝓuɪöċeαꝗ α
ꝗᵹαoɪleαö, ná α ᵹ-cuꝗ
ᵹo neɪṁníö, αċö beɪᴅ
öá ᵹ-cꝗáö le ᵹαċ uɪle
ꝓeαnαɪᴅ αᵹuꝗ ᴅoɪlᵹeαꝗ
ɪꝗ ꝓéɪᴅɪꝗ le céαċᴄαꝗ
αcα ᴅo ṁoċuᵹαö, no

They shall both be there
destroyed, both soul and
body, not dissolved or
reduced to nothing, but
afflicted with all the pain
and anguish that either
can be sensible of, and
able to endure. As the
rich man's body was so
tormented in that flame,

ᴏ'ꝼulᴀnᴣ. ₊Ⅿᴀp ᴏᴏ ƀí coᴘᴘ ᴀn ᴏúⅰne ꝶᴀⅰᴏƀⅰꝶ úᴏ ċoṁ moꝶ ꝶín ᴏá ᴘⅰᴀⅰᴀᴏ 'ꝶᴀn lᴀꝶᴀⅰꝶ, ᴣᴏ ꝶᴀⅰƀ ꝶe ᴀᴣ ⅰᴀꝶꝶᴀⅰᴏ ƀꝶᴀoⅰn uⅰꝶᴣe mᴀꝶ ᴏéⅰꝶc ċum ᴀ ċeᴀnᴣᴀ loⅰꝶᴣċⅰ ᴏ'ꝼuᴀꝶuᴣᴀᴏ, 'ꝶ ᴣᴀn ᴀn ƀꝶᴀon ꝼeⅰn ᴀꝶ ꝼᴀᴣᴀⅰl ᴀⅰᴣe : ᴀᴣuꝶ ᴣᴀċ ᴀ ꝶᴀċꝼuⅰᴏ ċum nᴀ h-áⅰᴄe úᴏ ᴏéⅰꝶ eⅰꝶeⅰꝶᴣe nᴀ ᴣ-coꝶꝶ beⅰᴏ 'ꝶᴀn loⅰmꝶᴣꝶⅰoꝶ ceᴀᴏnᴀ ꝶⅰn.

that he begged, but in vain, for a little water to cool his scorched tongue; so it shall be with all that shall be there after the resurrection of the body.

---

123. Ⱥꝶ ᴀn áᴏƀᴀꝶ ꝶⅰn, má'ꝶ cumᴀ lⅰƀ cᴀᴏ eⅰꝶeᴏ- ċᴀꝶ ᴏíƀ ᴏá éⅰꝶ ꝶo, ᴀꝶ ċonnꝶᴀᴏ ꝶóláꝶ ƀuꝶ b-peᴀcuⅰᴏe ƀeⅰċ ꝶeᴀl ᴀᴣuⅰƀ, ꝼeᴀᴏᴀⅰᴏ ꝶⅰƀ ᴏul ᴀꝶ ƀuꝶ n-ᴀᴣᴀⅰᴏ ᴀ ꝶⅰꝶ-ƀꝶⅰꝶeᴀᴏ ᴏlⅰᴣe ᴏé, le éᴀᴏóċuꝶ ⅰ n-ᴀ ᴣeᴀl- lᴀṁnᴀⅰƀ, ᴀᴣuꝶ le mᴀꝶ- luᴣᴀᴏ ᴀ ᴀnmᴀ nᴀoṁ- ċᴀ, ᴀᴣuꝶ le ꝼᴀⅰllⅰᴣe ᴏeᴀnᴀṁ ᴀ ꝶeⅰꝶƀⅰꝶ ƀuꝶ ᴣ-cꝶuċuⅰᴣċeóꝶᴀ uⅰle ċuṁᴀċᴄᴀⅰᴣ ; ᴀċċ bⅰoᴏ ᴀ ꝼⅰoꝶ ᴀᴣᴀⅰƀ ᴣᴏ ᴏ-ċíuƀ- ꝶᴀⱰⅰᴀ ċum ƀꝶeⅰᴄeᴀṁ- nuⅰꝶ ꝶⅰƀ um nᴀ neⅰċⅰƀ

Wherefore, if you care not what becomes of you hereafter, so you may but enjoy "the pleasures of sin for a season," you may still go on to transgress the laws, mistrust the promises, profane the name, and neglect the service of your Almighty Creator ; but "know that for all these things God will bring you into judgment," at the "great and terrible day of the Lord," and will then condemn you to that "everlasting pu-

ṗo uile, an lá moṗ
uaċḃáṗaċ úo aṗ o-Ꞇi-
ᵹeaṗna, aᵹuṗ ᵹo
n-oaimneoċaiḃ ṗé an
uaiṗ ṗin ṗiḃ ċum an
ṗionúiṗ ṗíoṗṗuiḃe úo,
oo ċualaḃaṗ anoiṗ,
aᵹuṗ moiċeoċaiḃ ṗiḃ
míle uaiṗe níoṗ meaṗa
iná ċualaḃaṗ, aᵹuṗ na
ṗéaoċaoi aṗmuaineaḃ.
Aċꞇ, ᵹloiṗ oo Ꝺhiá,
ṗéaouio ṗiḃ a ṗeaċnaḃ
ᵹo ṗeaḃ, má'ṗ áil liḃ
ṗéin: óiṗ aꞇá ṗiḃ a
ᵹ-coṁnuiḃe a o-ꞇal-
ṁain na m-béo, aᵹuṗ
aꞇá ᵹaċ uile ṗlíᵹe a-
ᵹuiḃ iṗ ṗéioiṗ o'iáṗ-
ṗuiḃ, le ḃ-ṗéaoṗuíḃe
ṗiḃ ṗéin oo ċonᵹḃail
ó ċuiꞇim ċum oaman-
ꞇa. Uime ṗin ᵹaḃaíḃ
coṁaiṗle uṗáio oo
ḃéanaṁ óioḃ coṁ ṗao
a'ṗ ṗéaoṗaíḃí ṗilliḃ ó'n
ꞇ-ṗlíᵹe ṗaiṗṗinᵹ úo oo
ṗeoluṗ ċum ḃaṗ n-oam-
anꞇa, aᵹuṗ oeanaiḃe
ṗúḃal, ó ṗo amaċ,
'ṗan ꞇ-ṗlíᵹe ċuṁainᵹ
úo ḃéaṗúṗ ṗiḃ ċum na
beaċa ṗioṗṗuiᵹe. lon-

nishment" which you
have now been hearing
of, and which you will
find to be far greater
than you have now heard,
or can yet imagine it to
be. But, blessed be God!
you are yet in a capacity
of avoiding it if you will;
for you are still in the
land of the living, and
have all the means that
can be desired, whereby
to prevent you "falling
into condemnation." Be
advised, therefore, to
make use of them while
you may, that you may
turn out of the way that
leads to destruction, and
walk for the future in
that narrow path that
will bring you to "life
everlasting;" that when
you come to stand be-
fore Christ's tribunal,
you may not be set at
his "left hand," and
from thence go into
"everlasting punish-
ment," but may be
found in the number of
the righteous, who shall

nuꞃ an ꞇꞃáꞇ ꞓiocꞃaíḋ
ċum ḃeiꞇ ann ḃúꞃ
ꞃeaꞃaḋ a láꞇaiꞃ ꞓa-
ꞇaoiꞃe ḃꞃeiꞇeaṁnuiꞃ
Chꞃioꞃꞇ, naꞓ ʒ-cuiꞃꞃi-
ḋeaꞃ ꞃiḃ aꞃ a láiṁ
ċlí, aʒuꞃ aꞃ ꞃin ʒo
ꞃeanuio ʒan ċꞃiꞓ, aꞓꞇ
ʒo m-beiḋ ꞃiḃ le ḃuꞃ
ḃ-ꞃaʒáil a n-uiṁiꞃ na
ḃ-ꞃíꞃéan ḃiáꞃ 'na ꞃea-
ꞃaḋ aꞃ a láiṁ ḋeiꞃ, a-
ʒuꞃꞃacꞃaꞃ aꞃ ꞃin ċum
na beaꞇa ꞃioꞃꞃuiḋe.
Ḃá ċóiꞃ ḋaṁ anoiꞃ
maꞃ an ʒ-céaona a
ꞇaiꞃbeanaḋ ḋíḃ cao
an ḃeaꞇa ꞃíoꞃꞃuiḋe
úo ċum a ꞃaċꞃúio na
ꞃíꞃeóin an lá ḋéiʒea-
naċ, maꞃ ḋeiꞃ an
bꞃeiꞇeaṁ, aꞓꞇ leiʒꞃiḋ
mé ꞃin ċoꞃam ʒo ṿ-ꞇi-
ʒiḋ aimꞃiꞃ oile.

stand on his "right hand," and go from thence into "life eternal." I should now, in like manner, shew what is that everlasting life, to which the righteous shall go in the last day, as the judge says, but I shall let that lie by until another occasion come.

124. Anoiꞃ ʒo ṿ-ꞇuʒaḋ Ḋia ṿ'á ʒꞃáꞃaiḃ ḋíḃ ꞃmuaineaḋ
ʒo ṿiꞇċeallaċ aꞃ a ʒ-cualaḃaꞃ ann ꞃo an uaiꞃ
ꞃe, aꞃ ṁoḋ ʒo ṿ-ꞇiuḃꞃaḋ ꞇoꞃaḋ uaiḋ ann ḃúꞃ
m-beaꞇa, aʒuꞃ ann ḃúꞃ n-ʒnioṁaꞃꞇaiḃ ċum naꞓ
m-beiꞇ baoʒal oꞃaiḃ an lá ḋeiʒeanaċ ṿul ċum an
ꞃionúiꞃ ꞃioꞃꞃuiḋe úo aꞃ a ꞃaiḃ me aʒ ꞇꞃáꞓꞇ liḃ,
aꞓꞇ ʒo m-beiꞇ ꞃiḃ ollaṁ ċum ṿul a meaꞃʒ na

ḃ-ḟiréan annṛ a' m-beaṫa ḟíoṛṛuiḋe. Ȝuíḋim Ḋia,
aȝuṛ iaṛṛáim, ṛo ḃ'aṫċuinȝe aiṛ, ṫṗé Íoṛa Chṛioṛṫ
áṛ ṛláṅuiȝṫeóiṛ aȝuṛ áṛ m-bṛeiṫeaṁ, ṛiḃṛe, aȝuṛ
miṛe ḃ' ḟaȝáil an lá moṛ úo annṛ a ṛṫaiḃ ṁaiṫ
ṛin. Ȝloiṛ, aȝuṛ úṁlaċṫ ḋó-ṛan, aȝuṛ ḋo'n aṫ-
aiṛ, aȝuṛ ḋo 'n Spioṛaḃ Naoṁṫa. Amen.

---

125. Ḋ'éiṛ ȝaċ neiṫe, iṛ le áṛ ȝ-cṛeiḋeaṁ a ȝ-Cṛioṛṫ
aṁáin, caiṫṗiȝṫeaṛ an ȝníoṁ ḃo nímiḃ, no ṛinn
ḟéin ḃo ní é, ḃeiṫ aṛ ȝabáil a ḃ-ḟíaḋnáiṛe Ḋé:
Oíṛ, ȝiḃ ḃ'é aṛ biṫ ḃo nímíḃ annṛ a' ṛṫaiḃ neiṁ-
ioṁláin ṛe, má ṫá ȝo n-ḋeanmaoiḃ é lé ȝṗá-
ṛaiḃ, aȝuṛ le conȝnaṁ Chṛíoṛṫ ḟéin; ȝiḃeaḃ maṛ
iṛ ṛinne ṛinne é, a ṫá ṛé ṛo-neiṁ-ioṁlán, aȝuṛ a
ḃ-ṛaḃ ó 'n ḃ-ḟiréanṫaċṫ ḋeaċṫuiȝeaṛ an ḃliȝeaḃ
oṛuinn: aȝuṛ uime ṛin ȝiḃ ḃ'é ḋeiȝ-ȝníoṁ a ṛaoilṫeaṛ a ḋéanaṁ linn, máṛ naċ ḃ-ḟuil ṛíṛ-ċeaṛṫ ȝo
h-ioṁlán, ní ḟéioiṛ meaṛ ṛiṛéán ḃo ḃeiṫ oṛuinne
aṛ a ṛon aȝ an Ḋia naċ ḃ-ḟuil cṛíoċ aṛ a ċṛíon-
aċṫ, ná aṛ a ḟíṛċeaṛṫ, ḃo ḃeiṛ bṛeiṫ aṛ ȝaċ uile
níḋ, ní ḃo ṛéiṛ maṛ ṛaoilṫeaṛ a m-beiṫ, aċṫ ḃo
ṛéiṛ maṛ aṫáiḃ ȝo ḋeiṁin ionṫa ḟéin: aċṫ ní ḟuil
ṛinne ḟíṛċeaṛṫ ȝo ḋeiṁin ionnáinn ḟéin, aȝuṛ uime
ṛin ni ḟéioiṛ meaṛ ḟíṛeanṫaċṫa ḃo ḃeiṫ oṛainn
aiȝe-ṛean ṛa aon níḋ ḃ'á ḃ-ḟuil ionáinn ḟéin; aċṫ
iṛ í an comṗoṛṫaċṫ aṫá aȝainn, ó ḃ'uṁluiȝ aon
mac Ḋe, ḃo ḃí ḟíṛéanṫa ȝo h-ioṁlán, é ḟéin ċum
báiṛ, eaḋon, báiṛ na cṛoiċe i n-áṛ náḋuiṛ-ne, aȝuṛ
aṛ aṛ ṛon, an ṁéiḃ ḃo ceanȝalṫaṛ ṛiṛ le cṛeiḋeaṁ
beoḋa maṛṫanaċ, aȝuṛ aȝa n-ḋeaṛnaḃ boill ḟíṛéán-
ṫa ḃ'á ċoṛṛ-ṛan ḃíoḃ maṛ ṛin, ȝo ḃ-ḟuil ceaṛṫ
aca aṛ a ḟíṛéanṫaċṫ ṛan, maṛ ȝuṛ leo ḟéin í; aȝuṛ

uime ṙin ᴄṗe na óeaᵹoiḃṗeaċa ṗan, aᵹuṗ ᴄṗé na
eaoaṗ-ᵹuióe aṗ a ṗon oo ᵹeiḃio meaṗ ṗíṗean a
láċaiṗ Oé ; maṗ iṗ cóiṗ oáiḃ, oo ḃṗiᵹ ᵹuṗ ab í
an ṗíṗéunᴄaċᴄ aᴄá aca ann-ṗan an ṗiṗeanᴄaċᴄ iṗ
iomláine ṗéaoúṗ aon ċṗéaᴄúiṗ 'ṗan ooṁan o'ṗá-
ᵹáil : aᵹuṗ aṗ ṗon naċ ḃ-ᵹuil ṗí ionnᴄa ṗéin, aċᴄ
ann-ṗan, iṗ leó-ṗan ann-ṗán coṁ maiᴄ aᵹuṗ oá
m-béiᴄ ṗi ionnᴄa ṗéin.

---

126. Maṗ ᵹeiḃ ṗinn an leiᵹion ṗo ó ṗéim an ᴄ-ṗoiṗᵹéil
ᵹo h-iomlán, ᵹeiḃmío ᵹo oíaṁṗaċ é ó naoṁ Pol,
oo ḃí ᵹan ṁilleán ann ᵹaċ uile ní ṗoiṗmeallaċ
ḃaineaṗ ṗiṗ an ḃ-ṗíṗéanᴄaċᴄ aᴄá 'ṗan olíᵹeao :
ᵹióeao oo ḃí a aċċuinᵹe oṗcionn ᵹaċ uile neiᴄe a
ṗaᵹail 'ṗan ᴄiᵹeaṗna Cṗioᴄ, ᵹan a ṗíṗeanᴄaċᴄ
ṗéin oo ḃeiᴄ aiᵹe ᴄáinic o'n olíᵹeao, aċᴄ an ṗíṗean-
ᴄaċo oo ᴄiᵹ ó ċṗeioeaṁ a ᵹ-Cṗíoᴄ, an ṗiṗeanᴄaċᴄ
aᴄá o Olia le cṗeioeaṁ.—Phi. iii. 6, 9. Aiᴄ a
ḃ-ṗeicmío é aᵹ laḃaiṗᴄ aṗ oá ᵹné o'ṗiṗeanᴄaċᴄ,
o'aoin ᵹné aca ᵹoiṗeaṗ ṗé aṗ ḃ-ṗiṗeanᴄaċᴄ ṗéin,
oo ᴄiᵹ o'n olíᵹeao, naċ ḃ-ṗéaoann ṗin oo óéanaṁ
ṗíṗeanᴄa, maṗ naċ ḃ-ṗuil ṗí iomlán, aᵹuṗ uime
ṗin, ní h-í aᴄá an ᴄ-aḃṗoal o'iaṗṗaio, nó, nió iṗ
cóṗa ṗáo, ní hí aṁáin i, iṗ ṗi an ᵹne oile, an ᵹne
aᴄa aᵹuinn ᴄṗé ċṗeioeaṁ a ᵹ-Cṗioᴄ, an ṗíṗeanᴄaċᴄ naċ ó óuine ᴄiᵹ, aċᴄ o óia, eaóon Oía aṗ
ṗlánuiᵹᴄeoiṗ, ᴄṗé ċṗeioeaṁ ann. Aᵹ ṗo an ṗiṗeanᴄaċᴄ aᴄá a n-Ioṗa Cṗioᴄ aᵹ na oaoiniḃ ċṗei-
oeaṗ ann, aᵹuṗ oo ṗaᵹᴄaṗ aṁluió ann-ṗan aᵹuṗ
léiᴄe ṗo, maṗ aᴄá ṗí ṗo iomlán oo niᴄeaṗ ṗíṗéanᴄa
iao, aᵹuṗ ᵹeiḃio meaṗ ṗíṗeanᴄaċᴄa a láċaiṗ Oé,
oo ṗéiṗ maṗ a oeiṗ an ᴄ-aḃṗᴄal céaona an áiᴄ

oıle ; maρ ıρ τρé eaρuṁlaċτ aon ouıne aṁáın oo
ρınneaò peacaıᵹeaċa oo ṁóρán, maρ an ᵹ-céaona ıρ τρé uṁlaċτ aon ouıne aṁáın eaòon Cρıoρτ,
oeanρuıᵹτeaρ ḟíρéın oo ṁóρán.—Rom. v. 19.

127. Aᵹuρ an ṁuınτıρ oo níτeaρ ᵹo oıonᵹṁalτa muρ
ρo ḟíρéanτa ıonnτa ḟéın,aᵹuρ ṁeaρτaρ ɓeıτ ḟıρean-
τa a ᵹ-Cρıoρτ, τρe na ᵹ-cρeıoeaṁ ann, maρ ᵹéaɓ
τaρ luċτ an ḟíρ-ċρeıoıṁ uıle an lá oeıᵹeanaċ,
ıρ ıao ρo na ḟíρéın oo ρaċḟáρ ċum na beaċa ρıoρ-
ρuıòé. Aᵹuρ ní ḟeıoıρ conτaɓaıρτ a òéunaṁ òe
ᵹo ρaċḟaıo ċum na beaċa ρıoρρuıòe, ó τáρla ḟocal
Chρıoρτ ḟéın ann ρo o'á òeaρɓaò òúınn.

128. Aċo ḟóρ, ní leóρ òúınn, a ċρeıoeaṁ maρ ρo, ᵹuρ
eaᵹ Cρíoρτ aρ ρon an ċıne òaonna ᵹo coıττean,
aċτ, ḟa òeoıò ıρ cóıρ oo ᵹaċ uıle òuıne a ċρeıoeaṁ
ᵹuρ eaᵹ ρé aρ a ρon ḟeın aᵹuρ aρ ρon a ρeacuıòe
ḟéın ᵹo ρρeρıálτa; aρ ṁoò ᵹo ᵹ-cuıρḟeaò aρ ḟuı-
lınᵹ Cρıoρτ annρ a' náòúıρ òaonna, òa ρeaρρúın
ḟeın aıτρıᵹe. Oıρ o τáρla ᵹo ρáıòτeaρ ᵹo ρoleıρ,
ᵹuρ ɓlaıρ Cρíoρτ an báρ aρ ρon ᵹaċ uıle òuıne,
ɓá cóıρ oo ᵹaċ uıle òuıne a ċρeıoeaṁ ᵹuρ ɓlaıρ
aρ a ρon ḟéın é. Eub. ii. 9. Aᵹuρ maρ naċ ḟéao-
oann aoın-neaċ ρo oo ċρeıoeaṁ, ᵹan aıτρıᵹe oo
òeanaṁ maρ an ᵹ-céaona, ní ḟéaoann aoın-neaċ
ρıoρ-aıτρıᵹe oo òéanaṁ ḟa n-a ρeacuıòıɓ uıle, naċ
ɓ-ḟeaoann, aᵹuρ naċ cóıρ oo ρo ċρeıoeaṁ, eaòon
ᵹuρ eaᵹ Cρıoρτ aρ a ρon ḟéın, aᵹuρ an ρon na
ɓ-peacuıòe ceaona ρın ḟa a n-oeaρna ρé aıτρıᵹe.
Maρ ρo ᵹeıɓmío naoṁ Pol aᵹ cuρ a ċρeıoıṁ a
n-ᵹnıoṁ, aṁáıl ıρ ɓeıτ aᵹ ρealɓuᵹao Cρıoρτ oo

féin. Táim ḋom ċéaraḋ, a ḋeip ré, pe Cpiopc;
giḋeaḋ atáim béo, aċt ní mé féin, aċt Cpíopc
atá béo ionnam; agup an beaṫa táim ag caiṫeaṁ
anoir 'pan ċolláinn, ip tpe ċpeiḋeaṁ ṁic Dé cai-
ṫim í, noċ ḋo ġpaḋuiġ mé, agup ḋo ċug e féin ap
mo pon.—Ġal. ii. 20.

---

129. Map po ġaċ ḋuine ḋo ní aiṫpiġe, agup ċpeiḋeap 'pan
t-poipġéal, ba coip ḋó a ṁeap gup ḋuine é féin
aga b-puil pealḃ ap leiṫ ann ġaċ niḋ ḋo pinniḋ,
agup ḋ' puiliġ Cpíopc ap pon an ċiniḋ ḋaonna,
ċoṁ móp áp ḋo ḋeanaṁ agup ḋ' puiliġpeaḋ é
aṁáin ap a pon féin: agup map pin atá ḋ'piaċaiḃ
opam-pa, agup map an ġ-céaḋna ap ġaċ ḋuine
oile, ni heaḋ aṁáin aoṁáil pe mo ḃéal, aċt a
ċpeiḋeaṁ ann mo ċpoiḋe, go n-ḋeápna pé ḋe féin
mac an ḋuine, ċum mac Dé ḋo ḋéanaḋ ḋíompa:
ḋo ġaḃ ap féin mo náḋuíp ḋaonna-pa, ċum go
m-beiṫ poinn agam-pa ḋ'á náḋúip ḋiaḋa-pan. Do
toipḃpeaḋ e ap pon mo ċionta pa, agup ḋo tóġḃaḋ
puap apíp é ċum mipi ḋo ḋéanaṁ pípeanta: Do
pinneaḋ peacaḋ ḋe ap mo pon pa ċum go n-ḋean-
taoiḋe pípeantaċt Dé ḋiom-pa ann-pan: ḋo éaġ pé
ċum go m-beinn-pe béo: agup ḋo ċéapaḋap ḋaoi-
ne é, cum go m-béiṫ glóip agam-pa maille le
Dhia go bpáṫ; óip ḋo ḃí gpáḋ aige opam, agup ḋo
ċug é féin ap mo pon. Agup uime pin anoip ó
ċápla go ġ-cuiṁníġim a ḃáp, agup ḋap leam, go
b-peicim ap an ġ-cpoiċ é, ní péaḋuim gan eiġeaṁ
go h-ápḋ, péaċ uan Dé tóġḃap leip peacaḋ an
ḋoṁain go coitċeann, agup mo peacuiḋepe ap
leiṫ.

130. Ⲁ Ioɼa ᵹⲣáⲃaiᵹ, a ⲩaiⲛ Ⲇé, ⲧóᵹⲃaɼ ⲣeacaⲃ aⲛ
ⲇoṁaiⲛ, oⲛoⲣaiⲙⲓⲟ ⲧú, aⲃⲣaiⲙíⲟ ⲧú, ⲧá ᵹⲣáⲃ
aᵹaiⲛⲛ oⲣⲧ, ⲟⲟ ⲥⲓⲟⲛⲛ ᵹⲩⲣ ᵹⲣaⲃⲩiᵹ ⲧú ⲣⲓⲛⲛ a ᵹ-céaⲟ-
óⲓⲣ, aᵹⲩⲣ ᵹⲩⲣ ᵹⲣaⲃⲩiᵹ ⲧú ⲥoṁⲙóⲣ ⲣⲓⲛ ⲣⲓⲛⲛ, ᵹⲟ
ⲟ-ⲧⲩᵹaⲓⲣ ⲧú ꝼéⲓⲛ aⲓⲣ áⲣ ⲣoⲛ. Ⲥaⲟ é aⲛ cⲩⲓⲟeaⲃa
ⲃéⲩⲣaⲙ ⲟⲩⲓⲧ, a Ⱦhláⲛⲩiᵹⲧeoⲓⲣ ⲣⲟ-ᵹⲣaⲃaiᵹ, ꝼáⲛ
ⲛᵹⲣáⲃ ᵹaⲛ eⲣíⲥ, aᵹⲩⲣ ꝼáⲛ ⲙⲩiⲛⲧeaⲣⲃaⲣ ⲣⲟ? Ⲁⲧá
a ꝼⲓⲟⲣ aᵹⲩⲓⲛⲛ ⲛaⲥ ⲃ-ꝼⲩiⲗ ⲧú aᵹ iaⲣⲣaⲓⲟ ⲛíⲟⲣ ⲙⲟ,
aᵹⲩⲣ ⲛí ꝼéaⲟⲙaoⲓⲟ-ⲛe ⲛⲓⲟⲣ lúᵹa ⲟⲟ ⲧaⲃaiⲣⲧ ⲟⲩⲓⲧ
ⲛá ᵹⲣáⲃ aⲓⲣ ᵹⲣáⲃ. Ⲁᵹ ⲣⲟ ⲩⲓⲙe ⲣⲓⲛ, aⲛ ⲛí ⲧá-
ⲙaⲟⲓⲟ ⲟⲟ ᵹeallaṁaⲓⲛ, aᵹⲩⲣ aⲧá ⲟⲟ ⲣúⲛ aᵹⲩⲓⲛⲛ a
ⲃéaⲛaṁ ⲣe ⲟⲟ ⲥoⲛᵹⲛaṁ ꝼéⲓⲛ. Ⲁᵹⲩⲣ aⲧáⲙaⲟⲓⲟ
ⲟⲟⲟ ᵹⲩⲓⲟe ⲥⲩⲙ aⲣ ᵹ-éⲣⲟⲓⲃⲧe ⲟⲟ líoⲛaⲃ, aᵹⲩⲣ ⲟⲟ
laⲣaⲃ ⲛíⲟⲣ ⲙó, aᵹⲩⲣ ⲛíⲟⲣ ⲙó ᵹaⲥ aoⲛ lá ⲣé ⲟⲟ
ᵹⲣaⲃ ꝼéⲓⲛ oⲣ cⲓⲟⲛⲛ ᵹaⲥ ⲩⲓle ⲛeiⲧe, ⲧⲣeⲣ aⲛ ⲛᵹⲣáⲃ
ᵹaⲛ ⲥoⲓⲙᵹe úⲟ ⲟⲟ ⲃí, aᵹⲩⲣ aⲧá ⲧú ⲧoⲓⲗⲧeaⲥ a ⲥaⲓⲣ-
ⲃeáⲛaⲃ ⲟúⲓⲛⲛ.

The Gloria in Excelsis.

131. Ᵹlóⲓⲣ ⲟⲟ Ⲇhⲓa aⲛⲛⲣ ⲛa ⲛeaṁaⲓⲃ ⲣⲟ-áⲣⲟa, aᵹⲩⲣ ⲣⲓoⲥ-
ⲥaíⲛ aⲣ aⲛ ⲧaⲗṁaⲓⲛ ⲟⲟ ⲛa ⲟáoⲓⲛⲓⲃ aᵹ a ⲃ-ꝼⲩiⲗ
ⲟeaᵹⲧoⲓl. Ⲙolaⲙaoⲓⲟ ⲧú, ⲃeaⲛⲛⲩiᵹⲙíⲟ ⲧú, ⲟⲟ
ⲃeⲓⲣⲙíⲟ ⲃⲩⲓⲟeaⲥⲩⲣ ⲟⲩⲓⲧ aⲣ ⲣoⲛ ⲟⲟ ṁóⲣ-ᵹlóⲓⲣe
ꝼéⲓⲛ, a ⲧⲓᵹeaⲣⲛa, a ⲣⲓᵹ ⲛeⲓṁe, a ⲟé, a aⲧaⲣ ⲛa
ⲛ-ⲩⲓle-cúṁaⲥⲧ.

Ⲁ Ⲧhⲓᵹeaⲣⲛa, a éⲓⲛ-ᵹⲓⲛ Ⲙhⲓc a ⲛ-Ⲁⲧaⲣ, a IOⲤⲀ
ⲤhⲢIOⲤⲦ, a Ⲧhⲓᵹeaⲣⲛa Ⲇⲓa, a ⲩaⲓⲛ Ⲇe, ⲟeaⲛ
ⲧⲣóⲥaⲓⲣe oⲣaⲓⲛⲛ, o'ⲣ ⲧⲩ ⲧóᵹⲃaⲣ ⲣeacⲩⲓⲃe aⲛ ⲟoⲙ-
aⲓⲛ, ᵹaⲃ éⲩᵹaⲟ aⲣ ⲛ-ⲩⲣⲛaⲓᵹe, ó'ⲣ ⲧú ꝼⲩⲓⲟeaⲣ aⲣ
láiṁ Ⲇé aⲛ aⲧaⲣ, ⲟeaⲛ ⲧⲣóⲥaⲓⲣe oⲣⲩⲓⲛⲛ, óⲓⲣ ⲓⲣ ⲧú
aṁáⲓⲛ aⲧá ⲛáoṁⲧa, ⲓⲣ ⲧú aṁáⲓⲛ aⲛ ⲧⲓᵹeaⲣⲛa, ⲓⲣ

H

τú aṁáιn ιr áιꞃ̇e, a IOSA CRIOST maιlle
leιr an Sꞃιoꞃaꞃ Naoṁ̇a a nꝣlóιꞃ Θé an Aṫaꞃ.
Amen.

––––––––––

Ꝣloιꞃ ꝺo'n Aṫaιꞃ, aꝣuꞃ ꝺo'n Mhac, aꝣuꞃ ꝺo'n Sꞃιo-
aιꝺ Naoṁ̇a ;
Maꞃ ꝺo b́í aꞃ ꝺ-τúr, aτá anoιr, aꝣuꞃ b́íaꞃ ꝣo bꞃaṫ.
Amen.

CHAPTER V.

READING LESSONS—CONSISTING OF SELECT PASSAGES FROM
THE HISTORY OF IRELAND, BY KEATING.

Sect. 1.—*Of the Lia Fail, or Stone of Destiny, brought into
Ireland by the Tuatha De Danann.*

Tuᵹaᴅaᴘ Tuaċa Ɖe Ɖanann leo ı n-Eıᴘınn ceıċᴘe ᴘeoı-ᴅe uaıᴘle maᴘ aᴄa, cloċ ó Faılıaᴘ, aᵹuᴘ ıᴘ ᴅı ᵹaıᴘmċeaᴘ an Lıa Faıl, aᵹuᴘ ıᴘ í ᴅo ᵹéımeaᴅ ᴘa ᵹaċ ᴘíᵹ Eıᴘıonn ᴘeıṁ beıċ aᵹ a ċoᵹaᴅ ᴅoıᴃ ᵹo h-aım-ᴘıᴘ Conċoᴃuıᴘ, aṁaıl a ᴅuᴃᴘamaᴘ ᴘoṁaınn ; aᴘ uaıċe ᴘoᴘ ᵹoıᴘċeᴘ Inıᴘ Faıl ᴅ'Eıᴘınn ; aᵹuᴘ ıᴘ ᴅo'n cloıċ ᴘın ᵹaıᴘmċeaᴘ cloċ na cıneaṁna, óıᴘ ᴅo ᴃí ı ᵹ-cıneaᴅ óí ᵹıbé áıᴄ ı n-a m-bíaᴅ an cloċ, ᴅuıne ᴅo cınneaᴅ Scuıᴄ, .ı. ᴅo ᴘıol Míleaᴅ Eaᴘ-páıne, ᴅo beıċ ı ᴃᴘlaıċeaᴘ na cᴘíċe ᴘın, ᴅo ᴘéıᴘ maᴘ léaᵹċaᴘ aᵹ *Hector Boethius*

The Thuatha De Danann brought with them into Ireland four precious rarities ; namely, a stone from Falias, called the Lia Fail, which used to roar under each king of Ireland upon his election, until the time of Connor, as we mentioned before. It is from it also that Ireland is called Innisfail. And it was the same stone that was called the stone of destiny, for it was destined for it, that wherever it should be placed, a person of the Scottish race, *i. e.* of the descendants of Milesius of Spain, should

ı ɼⱃaıɼ na h-Ⱥlban; aᵹ
ɼo maɼ a ꝋeıɼ·

be possessed of the sove-
reignty of that country
[Ireland], as we read in
Hector Boethius's His-
tory of Alban [*i. e.* Scot-
land]. Here are his words:

*" Ni fallat fatum, Scoti quocunque locatum
Invenient lapidem, regnare tenentur ibidem."*

Cınneaꝋ ɼcuıⱃ, ɼaoɼ an ꝼıne,

" The Scotic race, a noble
tribe,

ɱun buꝋ bɼéuᵹ an ꝼaıɼoıne,

Unless the prophecy be
false,

Maɼ a ɓ-ꝼuıᵹıꝋ an Ⱡıa Ꝼáıl,

Where they find the Lia
Fail,

Ꝋlıᵹıꝋ ꝼlaıⱦeaɼ ꝋo ᵹabáıl.

Empire there they've
right to assume "

Aɼ na ɱeaɼ ꝋo cıneaꝋ
Scuıⱃ an buaıꝋ ɼın ꝋo
ɓeıⱦ aᵹ an ᵹ-cloıc ɼın, ıaɼ
nᵹabáıl neıɼⱃ na h-Ⱥl-
ban ꝋ' Ꝼheaɼᵹuɼ ɱóɼ mac
Ɛaɼca, aᵹuɼ ıaɼ 'na cuɼ
ɼoıɱe ɼıᵹ Ⱥlban ꝋo ᵹaıɼm
ꝋe ꝼéın, cuıɼeaɼ ꝼıoɼ ı
n-ꝋáıl a ꝋeaɼbɼáⱦaɼ
Ɱhuıɼⱦeaɼⱃaıᵹ ɱıc Ɛaɼ-
ca, ꝋo ɼíol Ɛıɼıoɱóın, ꝼa
ɼıᵹ Ɛıɼıonn an ⱃan ɼın, ꝋ'á
ıaɼɼuıꝋ aıɼ an cloc ɼın ꝋo
cuɼ cuıᵹe ꝼéın ı n-Ⱥlbaın
ɼe ɼuıꝋe uıɼɼe ɼe h-uⱦⱃ
Rıᵹ Ⱥlban ꝋo ᵹaıɼm ꝋé;

The Scots being persuad-
ed that such power was
possessed by this stone,
Fergus the Great, son
of Erc, having subdued
the kingdom of Alban,
and being determined to
have himself proclaimed
king, sent an embassy
to his brother, Murtogh,
son of Erc, of the seed
of Eirevon, who was king
of Ireland at that time,
requesting him to send
him the stone to Alban
for him to sit upon at

agur ráinig an cloc map
rin é, agur do gaipmeað
Ríg Alban ap an g-cloic
óé. Agur ir e céað ouine
ðap gaipmeað pig Alban
do cineað Scuit é, agur
róp cap ceann go o-cug-
ẻaoi pioga Alhan ap cuio
do Cpuicneaċuib, .i. na
Picti, rul do píogað
Feapgur, maipeað ní pai-
be aon-pig iomlan oíob
gan beic ra cíor agur rá
cáin do píogaib Eipionn ó
aimrip go h-aimrip, agur
go h-aipigce ó aimrip
Eipeamóin mic Mileað
aleic, lép cuipeað na Picti
ð'áiciugað na h-Alban a
Laignib, amail a ðéapam
ðá éir ro ag labaipt ap
flaiceap Eipiomóin, go
flaiceap an Feapgura ro.

Dála na cloice, do bí aca
real aimripe oiaið i n-oi-
að, go ráinig ðá éir rin
go Sagroib, agur go

the time of his inaugu-
ration ; whereupon the
stone was sent to him,
and he was appointed
king of Alban upon it.
And he was the first
prince of the Scottish
race who was styled king
of Alban ; and, more-
over, although some of the
Cruithneans, i. e. Picts,
before the coronation of
Fergus, were styled kings
of Alban, yet there was
not one of them so inde-
pendently king, as not
to be under tax and tri-
bute to the kings of
Ireland, from time to
time, and especially from
the time of Eirevon, son
of Milesius, by whom the
Picts were sent out of
Leinster to settle in
Alban, to the reign of
this Fergus, as we shall
mention hereafter, in de-
tailing the reign of Eirevon.

As for the stone, they kept
it for many successive
ages, until at length it
found its way into Eng-

b-ꝼuıl ı n-oıu ꝼá'n ʒ-ca-
ċaoıꞃ ı n-a n-ʒaıꞃmċeaꞃ
Rıʒ Saʒꞃan, aꞃ 'na ċab-
aıꞃċ a h-Clbaın ʒo
h-aıṁóeonaċ a Maını-
ceaꞃ Scoıe, aʒuꞃ ıꞃ é an
ċéao Caobaꞃu ꞃí Saʒꞃan
ċuʒ leıꞃ í; ıonnuꞃ ʒuꞃ
ꞃíoꞃaó caꞃnʒaıꞃe na
cloıċe ꞃın 'ꞃan ꞃíʒ ꞃo a-
ʒuınn anoıꞃ, .ı. Séaꞃluꞃ,
aʒuꞃ ı n-a aċaıꞃ Rí Sea-
muꞃ ċáınıc oo ċıneaó
Scuıc, maꞃ a cá oo ꞃlıoċc
Máıne, ṁıc Cuıꞃc, ṁıc
Luʒóeaċ, ċáınıc ó Cıbeaꞃ,
ṁac Mıleaó Caꞃꞃáıne,
maꞃ ʒuꞃ ʒabaoaꞃ ʒaıꞃm
ꞃíʒ na Saʒꞃan aꞃ an
ʒ-cloıċ ꞃéaṁꞃáıóce.

land, where it remains to this day, under the throne on which the king of England is usually crowned, having been brought by force from Alban, from the abbey of Scone, by Edward I. king of England: so that the prediction respecting this stone has been verified in our present king Charles, and his father James (whose descent is of the Scottish race, namely, from' Mainy, son of Corc, son of Lovey, of the posterity of Eiver, son of Milesius of Spain), since they were crowned kings of England upon this stone.

SECT. 2.—*Of the Time of the Coming of the Milesians to settle in Ireland.*

C oeıꞃ Coꞃmac naoṁċa mac Cuıllennáın, aʒuꞃ Leabaꞃ' Ʒabála Cıꞃeann ʒuꞃ ab cuaıꞃım cꞃí ċé-ao oéaʒ blıaóaın ꞃoıṁ ChRIOSC cánʒaoaꞃ mıc Mıleaó ı n-Cıꞃınn. Cʒuꞃ

Holy Cormac Mac Cuillenain, and the Book of Conquests of Ireland, assert, that it was about 1300 years before Christ that the sons of Milesius came into Ireland. And

ατά *Polychronicon* αᴈ τεαὀτ
leo aη an áιηeaṁ ριn, maη
a ᴅ-τράὀτann aιη Éιηιnn ;
aᴈ ρo maη a ᴅeιη ; *ab ad-*
ventu Iberniensium usque
ad obitum sancti Patricii
sunt anni mille octingenti.
Ɑτaιᴅ (aη ρé) oὀτ ᴈ-céaᴅ
ᴅéaᴈ `blιaᴅaιn ó ὀoιᴅeaὀτ
na n-Éιηιonnaὀ ᴈo báη
Ρáττηaιc. Ionann ριn ηe
a ηaᴅa, aᴈuη ᴈuη ab τúaι-
ηιm τηí ὀéaᴅ ᴅéaᴈ blιa-
ᴅaιn ρul ηuᴈaᴅ CRIOSC
ὀánᴈaᴅaη mιc Mιleaᴅ ι
n-Éιηιnn; óιη baιn an ᴅá
blιaᴅaιn ᴅéaᴈ aᴈuη ὀeιτηe
ριὀιτ aιη ὀeιτηe ὀéaᴅ, ó
ᴈeιn ChRIOSC ᴈo báη
Ρáττηaιc, ᴅo na h-oὀτ
ᴈ-céaᴅ ᴅéaᴈ blιaᴅaιn úᴅ
áιηṁeaη *Polychronicon* ᴅo
beιὀ ó ὀoιᴅeaὀτ mac Mι-
leaᴅ ι n-Éιηιnn ᴈo báη
Ρáττηaιc, aᴈuη ᴅá ηéιη
ριn aτá oὀτ m-blιaᴅna aη
τηí ὀéaᴅ ᴅéaᴈ ó ὀoιᴅeaὀτ
mac Mιleaᴅ ι n-Éιηιnn ᴈo
ᴈeιn ChRIOSC ; ιonnuρ
ᴈo ᴅ-τιᴈ *Polychronicon*
aᴈuη Coηmac naoṁτa
Mac Cuιllenaιn aᴈuη na

the *Polychronicon* agrees
with them in this num-
ber, where it speaks of
Ireland. Here are its
words : [For the original
quotation see the ad-
joining column].
" There are," it says, "eighteen hundred years from
the coming of the Irish
to the death of Patrick."
This is the same as to
say that it was about
thirteen hundred years
before the birth of
Christ, that the sons of
Milesius came into Ire-
land : for, subtract ·the
492 years from the birth
of Christ to the death of
Patrick, from those 1800
years which the *Poly-*
chronicon enumerates as
having intervened be-
tween the coming of the
Milesians into Ireland
and the death of Pa-
trick, and there will con-
sequently remain 1308
years from the coming
of the Milesians into Ireland until the birth of

leabaᵽ ᵹabála ᵹo h-ıom-
lán ᵽe céıle.

Christ. So that the *Polychronicon*, and holy Cormac Mac Cuillenain, and the Book of invasions, entirely agree with one another.

Sᴇᴄᴛ. 3.—*Of the Coming of the Cruithneans or Picts to Ireland, their Battle with the Inhabitants, and Removal to Britain.*

Iᵽ ı b-ᵽlaıⱦeaᵽ Eıᵽeṁóın, ımoᵽᵽo, ⱦánᵹaɒaᵽ Cᵽuıⱦ-nıᵹ, .ı. *Picti,* ᵽluaᵹ ɒo ⱦᵽıall ó'n *Thracia,* ᵹo h-Eıᵽıᵽn, ɒo ᵽéıᵽ Coᵽ-maıc mıc Cuıllennáın ı n-a ᵽalⱦaıᵽ, aᵹuᵽ ᵹabaıɒ cuan aᵹ Inbeaᵽ Slaınᵹe. Cıᵹ *Beda* leıᵽ an nıö ᵽo, aⱦⱦ aṁáın ᵹo n-abaıᵽ ᵹuᵽ ab ᵽan leıⱦ ⱦuaıɒ ɒ'Eıᵽınn ⱦánᵹaɒaᵽ ı ɒ-ⱦıᵽ. Aᵹ ᵽo maᵽ a ɒeıᵽ 'ᵽan céaɒ ⱦaıbıoıl ɒo'n céaɒ leabaᵽ ᵽo ᵽcᵽíob ɒo ᵽⱦaıᵽ eaᵹ-laıᵽe Saᵹᵽan, *Contigit gentem Pictorum de Scythia (ut perhibent) longis navibus non multis Oceanum ingressam, circumagente flatu ventorum, extra fines omnes Britanniæ Hiberniam per-*

It was, moreover, in the reign of Eirevon, that the Cruithneans, *i.e.* Picts, a people of Thrace, came to Ireland (according to the account given by Cormac MacCuillenain in his Psalter), and landed in Slaney harbour. Bede agrees with this account, except that he says that it was in the north of Ireland they landed. Here is what he says in the first book that he wrote of the Church History of England. [See the adjoining column for the original Latin quotation, which will be found in Bede's *Hist. Eccles. Gentis Anglorum,*

venisse, ejusque Septentrionales oras intrasse, atque inventa ibi gente Scottorum, sibi quoque in partibus illius sedes petisse, nec impetrare potuisse. Τάρla vo ċιneaò na b-Ριcτ τeaċτ ó'n *Scythia* aṁuιl a veιρċeaρ, ι m-beaȝán vo loιnȝeaρ ρavo 'ρan oιȝéan ρe ρeolaò no ρe ρéιveaò na n-ȝaoċ τoιȝeaċτ leaċ a-muιȝ vo uιle ċeóρannuιb na òριoτaιne ȝo h-Θιριnn, aȝuρ aρ b-ρáȝaιl cιnιò Scuιτ ρompa, vo ιaρρavaρ ιonav coṁnuιve vóιb ρéιn ann ριn, aȝuρ ní b-ρuaιρeavaρ. Ȝιveaò ní ι v-τuaιρceaρτ Θιρeann τánȝavaρ ι v-τíρ, aċτ aȝ bun Ιnbιρ Slaιnȝe ι ȝ-cuan Loċa Ȝaρman, aṁaιl a vúbρamaρ. Aȝuρ ċaιnιc Cριoṁċann Scιaċbéal vo bí ι cceannuρ Laιȝean ó Θιρeaṁón an uaιρ ριn, ι n-a n-váιl ann ριn aȝuρ vo ριnne cáιρveaρ ριu. Ιρ ιav ρo ρa τaoιριȝ vo'n ċaòlaċ ριn, eaòon, Ȝuv aȝuρ a ṁac Caċluan, aȝuρ ιρ uιme

lib. i. cap. 1, the translation of which is as follows] :

"It happened that the Pictish race came from Scythia, as it is said, in a few long galleys, over the ocean, by the drift or blowing of the winds, into Ireland, passing outside all the British coasts. And finding the Scottish race before them, they asked for a settlement there for themselves, and did not obtain it." However, it was not in the north of Ireland they landed, but, as we have said, at the mouth of the River Slaney, in the harbour of Loch Garman [Wexford bay]. And Criffan Skeeavel, who was sovereign of Leinster at that time, under Eirevon, came to meet them there, and formed a friendship with them. The leaders of this expedition were Gud, and

oo ċeanȝail Cpioṁċann cáipoeap piu, oo ḃpíȝ ȝo paḃaoap oponȝa o'uaiplıḃ na ḋpeaċaıne, o'á n-ȝoıpċí Ɔuaċa Ƒıoóȝa, aȝ ȝaḃáıl neıpɔ ı ḃ-poċapɔaıḃ oo ȝaċ leıċ oo ḃun na Sláınȝe. Iȓ aṁlaıó oo ḃáoap an oponȝ pın, aȝuȓ nıṁ aıp apm ȝaċ aoın aca, ıonnuȓ máó beaȝ no móp an ċpeaċɔ oo ȝníċí leo, ní ȝaḃaó leıȝeap ap bıoċ ȝpeım oo'n oċap ȝo ḃ-ȓaȝaó báȓ, aȝuȓ oo ċuala Cpıoṁċann ȝo paıḃ opaoı oeıȝ-eolaċ o'á n-ȝoıpċí Ɔpopoán ı ḃ-ȓoċaıp na ȝ-Cpuıċneaċ oo ḃéapaó leıȝeap oo ȓéın, aȝuȓ o'á ṁuınnɔıp, a ȝ-coınne na nıṁe oo ḃıoó ap apmaıḃ Ɔuaċa Ƒíoóȝa, aȝuȓ oo ȓıaȓpaıȝ oo Ɔpopoán cpéao an leıȝeap oo óéanaó ı n-aȝaıó nıṁe apm na opoınȝe uo oo luaıóeamap. Cuıpċeap leaɔ ap Ɔpopoán, ɔpí ċaoȝao bo ṁaol ȓıonn o'á ȝ-cpúó, aȝuȓ cuıpċeap an laċɔ oo ȝéaḃɔap uaċa ı loȝ ap láp an ṁaċaıpe ı n-a

Cathluan, his son; and Criffan's reason for forming a friendship with them was, that there were certain British nobles, named Feehys, establishing themselves in Forth, on each side of the mouth of the Slaney. These people had all of them poisoned arms; so that whatever wound they inflicted, whether it were great or small, the patient received no benefit from medicine, but inevitably died; and Criffan heard that there was a very skilful druid among the Cruithneans, named Trosdan, who would give him a remedy for himself and his people, against the poisoned arms of the Feehys; and he accordingly asked Trosdan, what cure he was to use against the poisoned arms of the aforesaid people. Get milked 150 white cows without horns, said Trosdan, and let the milk taken from

ᵹcleaċċaⁿ liƀ ƀeiċ aᵹ
coṁpac ⱜiu, aᵹuⱜ ⱜóᵹaiⱜ
caċ oⱜⱜa aⱜ aⁿ maċaiⱜe
ᵹ-céaⱱna, aᵹuⱜ ᵹaċ aoⁿ
ⱱóⱱ ṁuiⁿⁿċiⱜ loiċⱜíⱱeaⱜ
leo, ċeiᵹeaⱱ 'ⱜaⁿ loᵹ ⱱ'a
ⱜoċⱜaᵹaⱱ, aᵹuⱜ buⱱ ⱜláⁿ
ó ᵹoiⁿ ⁿa ⁿiṁe é. ⱱo
ᵹⁿíċeaⱜ le Cⱜioṁċaⁿⁿ a
ⁿ-ⱱuƀaiⱜċ aⁿ oⱜaoi, aᵹuⱜ
ⱜóᵹⱜaⱜ caċ Aⱜⱱa leaṁ-
ⁿaċċa aⱜ Ċuaċaiƀ Ⱇioⱱ-
ᵹa, aᵹuⱜ bⱜiⱜeaⱜ ⱱóiƀ ᵹo
ⱱ-ċuᵹ a ⁿ-ⱱeaⱜᵹ-áⱜ aⁿⁿ.

ⱱála ⁿa ᵹ-Cⱜuiċneaċ aⁿⁿ
ⱜiⁿ, maⱜ a ċa Ᵹuⱱ aᵹuⱜ
Caċluaⁿ a ṁac, cuiⱜiⱱ
ⱜómⱜa ⁿeaⱜċ Ɫaiᵹeaⁿ ⱱo
ᵹaƀail, aᵹuⱜ maⱜ ⱱo ċua-
laiⱱ Eiⱜeaṁóⁿ ⱜiⁿ, ċionó-
luⱜ ⱜluaᵹ líonṁaⱜ, aᵹuⱜ
ċiᵹ ⱱ'á ⁿ-ioⱜⱜaiᵹe, aᵹuⱜ
maⱜ ⱱo ċoncaⱱaⱜ ⁿa
Cⱜuiċniᵹ ᵹaⁿ iaⱱ ⱜéiⁿ
líoⁿ caċuiᵹċe ⱜiⱜ ceaⁿᵹ-
laiⱱ ⱜíċ aᵹuⱜ cáiⱜⱱeaⱜ
ⱜiⱜ. Noċċaⱜ Eiⱜeaṁóⁿ
ⱱóiƀ ᵹo ⱜaiƀe ⱱúċaiⱱ ⱱo'ⁿ
leiċ ċoiⱜ ċuaiⱱ ⱱ' Eiⱜiⁿⁿ

them be put in a pit in the middle of the field where you are accustomed to fight with them, and provoke them to battle there, and every one of your people that is wounded by them, let him bathe in the pit, and he shall be healed from the poisoned wound. Criffan acted according to the Druid's advice, and proclaimed the battle of Ardlennachta against the Feehys, and there defeated them with bloody slaughter. As for the Cruithneans then, namely, Gud and his son Cathluan, they determine to seize upon Leinster; and when Eirevon heard this, he assembles a numerous army, and proceeds against them. But the Cruithneans, perceiving that they were not of themselves able to fight them, made peace and friendship with him. Eirevon informs them

αֵ֖ur α ouƀαιрτ ֵpιu oul o'α n-άιτιuֵ֖αὀ. Ιֵ֖ απη ֵpιη oo ιαֵֵ֖pαoαֵ֖ Cֵ֖uιτnιֵ֖ αֵ֖ Eιֵ֖ea֟món cuιo oo na mnάιƀ uαιֵ֖le oo ƀί ι n-αonτu֟ha αιֵ֖e ֵ֖é׀η oo ֟hnάιƀ na o-ταoιֵ֖eaֵ֖ τάι-nιc leó ó'n Eαֵֵ֖pάιη, oάֵ֖ mαֵ֖ƀαὀ α ƀ-ֵpιֵ֖, oo ταƀ-αιֵ֖τ oóιƀ ֵ֖eιη, oo ֵ֖eιֵ֖ *Beda* ֵ֖απ ֵ֖éαo ֵ֖αιƀιoιl oo'n ֵ֖éαo leαƀαֵ֖ oo ֵ֖ταιֵ֖ na Sαֵֵ֖pαη, αֵ֖uֵ֖ oo ֵ֖eαn-ֵ֖lαoαֵ֖ ֵ֖άτα Ꙅֵ֖éιne αֵ֖uֵ֖ Eαֵ֖cα oֵֵ֖pα ֵ֖eιη ֵ֖uֵ֖ ab mó oo ƀιαὀ ֵpιoֵ֖αֵ֖τ Cֵ֖uιֵ֖ean-τuαֵ֖, ֵpιֵ֖ α ֵ֖άιὀτeαֵ֖ Αlbα ι n-oιu, αֵ֖ α ֵ֖ealbúֵ֖αὀ ó ƀαֵ֖άnτuֵ֖ ֵpleαֵ֖τα na m-ban ιnά ó ƀαֵ֖αnnτuֵ֖ ֵpleαֵ֖τα na ƀ-ֵ֖eαֵ֖, ֵ֖o cֵ֖íֵ֖ an ƀeαֵ֖α. Ꞇuֵ֖ Eιֵ֖ea֟món aֵ֖ an n-αֵ֖τ ֵpιη τֵ֖ιúֵ֖ ban oóιƀ .ι. bean Ꙅֵ֖eιֵ֖ι, bean ƀuαιֵ֖, αֵ֖uֵ֖ bean ƀuαιֵ֖ne, αֵ֖uֵ֖ ֵ֖αƀuֵ֖ Cαֵ֖luαη ֵ֖α άֵ֖o-ταoιֵ֖eaֵ֖ oóιƀ, bean oíoƀ oo ֵ֖éιη. Ꞇֵ֖ιαlluιo ann ֵpιη ֵ֖o Cֵ֖uιֵ֖ean-τuαֵ֖, αֵ֖uֵ֖ oo ֵ֖αƀ Cαֵ֖luαη neαֵ֖τ na cֵ֖íֵ֖e ֵpιη, αֵ֖uֵ֖ ֵ֖α h-é ֵ֖éαo ֵ֖íֵ֖ Αlbαη oo

that there was a country north-east of Ireland, which he advised them to go and settle in. Upon this the Cruithneans asked Eirevon for some of the women who were marriageable, of those that were with him, of the wives of the chiefs who came with them from Spain, whose husbands had been killed (according to Bede, in the first chapter of the first book of the History of the English). And they bound themselves by the ties of sun and moon, that the sovereignty of the Cruithnean country, now called Alban, should be rather possessed in right of the female than the male descent for ever. Eirevon, upon this condition, gave them three women, namely, the wife of Bres, the wife of Buas, and the wife of Buaney. And Cathluan, who was their principal leader, took

Chꞃuꞁcneaċaꞁꞇ e, aṁaꞁl
leaᵹcaꞃ ꞁꝈꞃalcaꞁꞃChaꞁꞃꞁl,
'ꞃan ꝺuaꞁn ꝺáꞃ ab copaċ,
"Ꝺ eolċa Ꝺlban uꞁle."

one of these for himself.
They then departed for
the Cruithnean country,
and Cathluan seized the
sovereignty there, and
was the first king of Al-
bany of the Cruithnean
race, as we read in the
Psalter of Cashel, in the
poem beginning "Ye
learned of Alba all."

SECT. 4.—*Of Ollamh Fola, and the Convention, or Feis, of Tarah; instituted by him.*

Ꝺo ᵹaꞇ Ollaṁ Ꝼoꞃla, mac
Ꝼꞁaċaꞁꝺ Ꝼꞁonꞃcocaꞁᵹ ꞃꞁoᵹ-
aċc Ꞓꞁꞃeann cꞃꞁoċaꝺ blꞁa-
ᵹaꞁn, aᵹuꞃ a éuᵹ 'na muꞃ.
Iꞃ uꞁme ᵹoꞁꞃċeaꞃ Ollaṁ
Ꝼoꞃla ꝺe, ꝺo ꞇꞃꞁᵹ ᵹo
ꞃaꞁꞇe 'n-a ollaṁ a ꞇ-ꝼꞁlꞁ-
ꝺeaċc, aᵹuꞃ a n-eaᵹna,
aᵹuꞃ ꞁ n-eoluꞃ ꞃe ꞃeaċ-
coꞁꞇ, aᵹuꞃ ꞃe ꝺlꞁᵹċꞁꞇ
ꝺ'óꞃꝺuᵹaꝺ ꞁ n-Ꞓꞁꞃꞁnn ꞁ n-a
ꞃé, aᵹuꞃ ꞁꞃ leꞁꞃ ꝺo ꞃꞁnneaꝺ
Ꝼéꞁꞃ Ꞓeaṁꞃac aꞃ ccuꞃ ꞁ
n-Ꞓꞁꞃꞁnn.

Ollav Fola, son of Fiachy
Finscotha, reigned over
Ireland thirty years, and
died in his own house.
He was called Ollav
Fola, because of his be-
ing accomplished in phi-
losophy, and wisdom,
and in understanding of
laws, and in settlement
of statutes in Ireland in
his days, and it was by
him the Feis of Tara was
first established in Ire-
land.

Ionann ꞁomoꞃꞃo Ꝼeꞁꞃ Ꞓeaṁ-
ꞃaċ aᵹuꞃ ꞃꞁoᵹꝺaꞁl ċoꞁc-
ċꞁonn aṁuꞁl *Parliament*,
maꞃ a ccꞁᵹᵹaꝺ coꞁ ṁċꞁonól

The Feis of Tara was the
same as a royal conven-
tion, like a Parliament,
in which the nobles and

uaṗal aᵹuṗ ollaṁan Ein-
eann ᵹo Ceaṁṗaiᵹ ᵹaċa
ṫṗeaṗ bliaὸain um Shaṁ-
ḟuin maṗ a ᵹ-cleaċṫaoi
leo ṗeaċṫa aᵹuṗ oliᵹċe
o'aċnuaὸúᵹaὸ, aᵹuṗ o'oṗ-
oúᵹaὸ, aᵹuṗ ḟṗoṁaὸ oo
ὸéanaṁ aiṗ ḟeanċuṗ aᵹuṗ
aṗ ḟeanoala Eiṗionn. Iṗ
ann ḟóṗ oo h-oṗouiᵹeaὸ
ionao ṗuiὸe oo ᵹaċ ceann
ḟeaὸna oá m-bioὸ oṗ
cionn na laoċṗuiὸe oo
bioὸ aiṗ buannaċṫ aᵹ
ṗíoᵹaiḃ aᵹuṗ aᵹ ṫiᵹeaṗ-
naὸuiḃ Eiṗeann. Oo bioὸ
ḟóṗ oo nóṗ i ḃ-ḟéiṗ Ceaṁ-
ṗaċ, ᵹibe oo ὸéanaὸ ᵹoio,
oo buaileaὸ neaċ, no o'im-
ṗeaὸ aṗm aiṗ, báṗ oo
ċaὸaiṗṫ oo, aᵹuṗ ᵹan
neaṗṫ aᵹ an ṗíᵹ ḟéin, ná
aᵹ aon eile maiṫṁeaċaṗ
oo ṫaὸaiṗṫ 'ṗan ᵹníoṁ ṗin
oo. Oo cleaċṫaoi ḟóṗ leo
beiċ aiṗ ḟeaὸ ṗé lá aᵹ
coṁól ṗul oo ḟuiὸeaὸ an
ṗíaᵹὸáil, maṗ aṫá, ṫṗí lá
ṗoiṁ Shaṁuin, aᵹuṗ ṫṗí
lá o'á h-éiṗi aᵹ ṗnaὸmaὸ
ṗíoċċána aᵹuṗ aᵹ cean-
ᵹal cáiṗoeaṗa ṗe céile.

learned of Ireland used
to meet every third year
at Tarah, at the Feast of
Samhuin ; and in which
they used to reform and
settle acts and statutes,
and regulate the annals
and records of Ireland.
Here also there was a
seat assigned to each of
the generals who com-
manded the armies in
the service of the kings
and rulers of Ireland. It
was also a rule at the
Feis of Tara, that who-
soever committed a rob-
bery, or struck or as-
saulted any one, should
suffer death, without the
king himself, or any
person else, having power
to pardon the crime.
They used also to as-
semble and enjoy festi-
vity together six days
before the sitting of the
council, that is three
days before the Feast of
Samhuin, and three days
after it, thus confirming
peace and establishing
friendship with one ano-
ther.

Sᴇᴄᴛ. 5.—*Enumeration of the Episcopal Sees in Ireland.*

Ατάιο ceιτ̇пe h-αιпоeαрbοιჳ ι n-Єιпιnn, map α τα, Αпоeαрbοჳ Αпоαmαċα, Pпιοṁғαιὸ nα h-Єιпeαnn uιle, Αпоeαрbοჳ Ατ̇α-clιατ̇,Αпоeαрbοჳ Chαιпιl, αჳuр Αпоeαрbοჳ Τhuα-mα.

Ιр ға'n Pпιοṁ ғαιὸ αταιο nα h-eαрbuιჳ ро пίoр; Єαр-bοჳ nα Mιὸe, no οο пeιп *Cambden*, Єαрbοჳ Αιl nα Mίпeαnn, .ι. Uιпneαċ, oιп ιр αιnm οο'n lίჳ ατα ι n-Uιпneαċ Αιl nα Mι-пeαn; ιοnαnn ιοmoппο Αιl αჳuр lιαჳ no cloċ, αჳuр· οο bпιჳ ჳuр αb ι αn ċloċ пιn αn τeoпα ιοιп nα ceιτ̇-пe ċοιჳeαὸαιb ο'αп bαιn-eαὸ nα ceιτ̇пe mιпe ο'ά n-οeαпnαὸ αn Mhιὸe, οο ჳοιпeαὸ Αιl nα Mίпeαnn οί, αჳuр ჳοιпτ̇eαп leαc nα ჳ-coιჳeαὸ mαп αn ჳ-céαο-nα οί; Єαрbοჳ Ὀhúιn-οα-leαċ-ჳlαп, Єαрbοჳ Chloċ-αιп, Єαрbοჳ Chuιnnιпe, Єαрbοჳ Αпоαċαιὸ, Єαр-bοჳ Rαċα-bόċ, Єαрbοჳ

There are in Ireland four archbishops, viz. : the Archbishop of Armagh, Primate of all Ireland ; the Archbishop of Dublin ; the Archbishop of Cashel ; and the Archbishop of Tuam. Under the primate are the following bishops : the Bishop of Meath, or, according to Cambden, the Bishop of Ail na Mireann, i. e. Uishnagh ; (for *Ail* is the same as *flag* or *stone*, and on account of that stone being the boundary between the four provinces, from which were taken the four portions of which Meath was composed, it was called *Ail na Mireann* [i. e. the stone of the portions], and it was also called the provincial stone ;) the Bishop of Dun-da-leth-glas, [i. e. Down] ; the Bishop of Clogher ; the Bishop of Connor ; the

Raᴄa ᴌuｐaιᵹ, Єaｒboᵹ
Ohaιlmocaιｐ, Єaｒboᵹ
Ohoιｐe.

Bishop of Ardagh ; the
Bishop of Raphoe ; the
Bishop of Rath Luc; the
Bishop of Dalmochar ;
the Bishop of Derry.

Fá Cｐoeaｒboᵹ Cᴄa-clιaᴄ
aᴄa Єaｒboᵹ Ƶhlιnne ᴅá
loᴄa, Єaｒboᵹ Feaｐna,
Єaｒboᵹ Oｐｐaιᴅe, Єaｒboᵹ
ᴌeιᴄ-ᵹlιnne, aᵹuｐ Єaｒboᵹ
Chιlle-ᴅaｐa.

Under the Archbishop of
Dublin are: the Bishop of
Glendalough; the Bishop
of Ferns ; the Bishop of
Ossory ; the Bishop of
Leighlin; and the Bishop
of Kildare.

Fa Cｐoeaｒboᵹ Chaιｐιl aᴄá
Єaｒboᵹ Chιlle ᴅa ᴌua,
Єaｒboᵹ ᴌuιmnιᵹ, Єaｒboᵹ
Innｐe Caᴄaιᵹ, Єaｒboᵹ
Chιlle Fιonnaḃｐaᴄ, Єaｒ-
boᵹ Imlιᵹ, Єaｒboᵹ Roｐa
Cｐé, Єaｒboᵹ Phuιｐᴄ-
laιｐᵹe, Єaｒboᵹ ᴌeaｐa
Mhóιｐ, Єaｒboᵹ Chluana,
Єaｒboᵹ Coｐcaιᵹe, Єaｒ-
boᵹ Ruιｐ ua Caιｐbｐe,
aᵹuｐ Єaｒboᵹ Cｐoa Feｐ-
ᴄa.

Under the Archbishop of
Cashel are: the Bishop of
Killaloe ; the Bishop of
Limerick; the Bishop of
Inniscathy ; the Bishop
of Kilfenora; the Bishop
of Emly ; the Bishop of
Roscrea; the Bishop of
Waterford ; the Bishop
of Lismore ; the Bishop
of Cloyne; the Bishop of
Cork ; the Bishop of
Rosscarbery ; and the
Bishop of Ardfert.

Fa Cｐoeaｒboᵹ ᴄuama aᴄa
Єaｒboᵹ Chιlle mιc Ouaᴄ,
Єaｒboᵹ Mhuιᵹe-eo, Єaｒ-
boᵹ Єanaᴄ Ouιn, Єaｒboᵹ
Chιlle Iaｐᴄaιｐ, Єaｒboᵹ
Roｐa Comaιn, Єaｒboᵹ

Under the Archbishop of
Tuam are : the Bishop
of Kilmac-duagh ; the
Bishop of Mayo ; the Bi-
shop of Enachdun ; the
Bishop of Kill-Iarthar ;

Chluana Feprca, Earbog Aċaıḃ Conaıpe, Earbog Chılle Alaḃ, Earbog Chonaınne, Earbog Chılle Monuaċ, aȝur Earbog Aıle-fınn.

the Bishop of Roscommon; the Bishop of Clonfert; the Bishop of Achonry; the Bishop of Killala; the Bishop of Conainn; the Bishop of Kill-mo-nuach; and the Bishop of Elphin.

Ir í aoır an Cıȝeapna, ɔo peır *Cambden*, an can ɔo h-ópouıȝeaḃ na ceıċpe apɔeapboıȝ ı n-Eıpınn míle, céaɔ, aȝur ɔa bliaȝaın aıp ḃa fıċċeaɔ.

The year of our Lord in which the four archbishops were appointed in Ireland, was, according to Cambden, 1152.

Ɔo ċuıp mé mopan eapbog ann ro ríor, aıp lopȝ *Cambden*, nac ḃ-fuıl ap conȝḃaıl anoır, na caċaoıp Earboıȝ ınnce, aċc ıaɔ ap n-a ȝ-cup ap ccúl, aȝur cuıɔ eıle ap n-a ȝ-ceanȝal ɔ'a ċeıle ḃíoḃ, aȝur ap n-a ccup fa aon-Earbog, map acá Cıopmop aȝur Popclaıpȝe fa aon-eapbog, Cluaın aȝur Copcaıȝ fa aon eapbog eıle, aȝur mup rın ɔoıḃ ó foın amaċ.

I have set down here from Cambden, several bishops that do not now exist, and for whom there are no episcopal cities, some of them having been suppressed, and some of them united to others, and placed under one bishop; as, for instance, Lismore and Waterford, under one bishop; Cloyne and Cork, also under one bishop; and so of the rest.

Sᴇᴄᴛ. 6.—*Of Nial Naoighiallach, Monarch of Ireland, his Expedition to Scotland and France, and Capture of St. Patrick.*

Αοιρ Τιχεαρρα 377. Ꝺo χαƀ Nιαll Nαοιχιαllαċ, mαc Єoċαιƀ Мuιχṁeαƀοιn, ꝺo ṗíol Єιριοṁοιn, ριοχαċo Єιρeαnn 27. m-bliαƀnα. Αρ é αn Nιαll ρo ꝺo ċuαιƀ χo ρluαιχ lιonṁαρ mαιlle ριρ ꝺo neαρτuχαƀ αχuρ ꝺo ρρeαṁuχαƀ Ꝺhαlρíαꝺα αχuρ ċιnneαƀ Scuιτ ι n-Αlboιn, ꝺo ƀí ρά'n αm ροιn α χαƀαιl neιρτ αρ Chρuιτneαċαιƀ ꝺ'á n-χοιρτι Ριcτι; αχuρ ιρ é céαꝺ ꝺuιne τuχ Scotia ꝺ'αιnm αρ Αlbαιn é, αρ ιmριƀe Ꝺhαlρıαꝺα, αχuρ ċιnneαƀ Scuιτ, αρ coιnχιoll χo m-bo Scotia Minor, no Scotia bα lúχα ꝺo ƀeαρρτάοι uιρρe, αχuρ Scotia Major, .ι. Scotia αρ mo ꝺo χοιρρıƀe ꝺ-Єιριnn.

Α ꝺeιρ ρορ Nennius, uχꝺαρ ƀρeατnαċ, ꝺo ρeιρ Cambden, χuρ αb ραn ceατραṁαƀ h-αοιρ ꝺo χαƀαꝺαρ nα Scythia .ι. cιnneαƀ Scuιτ ρeαlƀ nα h-Єιρeαnn. Αρ ρolluρ ρορ α h-αnάluιƀ Єιρeαnn χuρ αb Αlbα ρα h-αιnm ꝺon ċρıċ χo h-αιmρıρ Neιll Nαοιχιαllαċ, αχuρ mαρ ρuαραꝺαρ Ꝺαlρıαꝺα Scotia ꝺo ċαƀαιρτ αρ Αlbα, ꝺo leαnαꝺαρ ρeιn αχuρ α ρlιoċτ ꝺo'n αιnm o ρuιn αleιċ: Ɠıƀeαƀ Ɠαοƀeιl Єιρeαnn ꝺo coıṁeαꝺαꝺαρ αn τ-αιnm ρuαραꝺαρ ρompα αρ αn c-ċρıċ, .ι. Αlbα; αχuρ ιρ e ριn χαιρmıꝺ ρeιn αχuρ α ρlιoċτ ꝺı. Rοıṁe ριn ιomορρο *Alba* no *Albania* ρα h-αιnm ƀı, o *Albanactus* αn τρeαρ mαc ꝺo *Brutus*, οιρ αρ í Αlbα ραιnıc muρ ċuιꝺ ρonnα ꝺo ó n-α αċαιρ.

Τρıuρ mαc ιomορρο ꝺo ƀı αχ *Brutus*, ꝺo ρeιρ *Monomotensis*, mαρ ατα *Laogirius, Camber*, αχuρ *Albanactus;* αχuρ ꝺo ρoιnn *Brutus* οιleαnn nα ƀρıοταιne móıρe eατορρα, αχuρ ċuχ ꝺo *Laogirius, Laogria*, ατα αρ nα ρloιnneαƀ uαιƀ ρeιn; αχuρ αρ οι χαιρτeαρ *Anglia* αnıu.

ᴄuᴣ ᴅo *Camber, Cambria,* ᴅa n-ᴣoιρᴛeaρ ᴅρeaᴛaιn
anιu; aᴣuρ an ᴛρeaρ míρ ᴅo *Albanactus,* o ᴛᴛuᴣᴛaρ
Albania aρ ᴄlboιn.

ᴄeιᴅ Nιall ᴅa eιρ ριn ᴣo h-ᴄlboιn ᴣo *Laogria* lía n-a
ρ̇luaιᴣ, aᴣuρ ᴅo ριnne ρoρlonᴣρoρᴛ ιnnᴛe, aᴣuρ cúιρ-
eaρ caᴃlaċ ᴣo ᴅρeaᴛoιn na Ƒρaιncᴣe ᴅa n-ᴣoιρᴛeaρ
Armorica, ᴅaρccoιn na cριċe ᴣo ᴛᴛuᴣaᴅaρ ᴅá ċeúᴅ
ᴃρaιᴣᴅe ᴅo leanᴃ uaιρle leo ι n-Ɵιριnn; aᴣuρ ιρ aρ
m-ᴃρoιoριn ᴛᴛuᴣaᴅaρ Ρaᴛᴛρuιc leo an aoιρ a ρ̇e
m-ᴃlιaᴣaιn ᴅéaᴣ, aᴣuρ ᴅá·ρ̇ιaιρ ᴅo, maρ aᴛa *Lupita*
aᴣuρ *Darerca,* aᴣuρ ιomaᴅ ᴅo ᴃρaιᴣᴅιᴃ oιle aρ ċeann.

Ⱬeuᴣᴛaρ lιnn ι m-beaċa Ρhaᴛᴛρuιc ρuaρamaρ ρᴣριoᴃċa
ι ρeanleaᴃaρ Meambρuιm maρaon ρe beaċa Mocu-
ᴅa, aᴣuρ ᴄbbáιn, aᴣuρ naoṁ oιle ᴣuρ ab ᴅρeaᴛnaċ
Ρaᴛᴛρuιc. ᴄᴣ ρo bρíaċρa an ᴛ-ρeínleaᴃáιρ. *Patricius Britto, natus in oppido Nempthor, in campo Taburno
.ι. Tabernaculorum, ex parentibus religiosis ortus.* Ρaᴛᴛρuιc (aρ ρe), ᴅρeaċnaċ aρ na bρeιċ ρan m-baιle ᴅaρ
ab aιnm Neamᴛoρ ι Maᴣ na ᴃ-ριanᴃoċ ó ċuιρᴛιᴣċιᴃ
cρaιᴃċeaċa ᴅιaᴅa.

ᴄ ᴅeιρ aριρ ρan aιᴛ ċeaᴅna na bρíaċρaρo. *Cum Scoti de
Hibernia sub rege suo* Nιall-naoι-ᴣιallaċ *diversas pro-
vincias Britanniæ contra Romanorum imperium multum
devastabant contendere incipientes aquilonalem Britanniæ
plagam, tandem ejectis veteribus colonis ipsi Hibernienses
eam occupaverunt et habitaverunt.* Ιaρ naρccoιn ιomoρ-
ρo ιomaᴅ cριoċ ρan ᴅριoᴛaιnne ᴅo *Scotaiᴃ* ó Ɵιρe
maρ aon ρé na ριᴣ ρeιn Nιall náoιᴣιallaċ a n-aᴣaιᴅ
ρlaιċιoρ na Roṁa, ᴅo haιρcceaᴅ ᴣo móρ an ᴅhρíoᴛaιnne
leo: aρ ᴛuρ an leιċ ċuaιᴅ ᴅι; aᴣuρ ιaρ n-ᴅι-
bιρᴛ na ρean-ροιρne aιρᴛe ᴅ'áιᴛιᴣeaᴅaρ Ɵιριonᴅa ρeιn
ιnnᴛe. ᴄ ᴅeιρ an ᴛ-úᴣᴅaρ ceaᴅna ρan aιᴛ ceaᴅna ᴣo
ᴛᴛaιnιc ᴅe ρo ᴛρí Ríoᴣaċᴛa ᴅo ᴃeιċ ρan m-ᴅριoᴛaιn

ṁoıp, maṗ aʐa *Scotia, Anglia, et Britannia.* Ɑ ɒeıp
an ʐ-uᵹɒaṗ ceaɒna ᵹuṗ ab ḟa'n amṗo, aṗ m-beıʐ ɒo
Nıall Náoıᵹıallaċ ṗan eaċʐpa ṗo aᵹ planòuᵹaɓ ɒal-
ṗıaɒa ı n-Ɑlboın ɒo ċuaıɓ coɓlaċ Єıṗıonnaċ ɒo'n aıʐ
ına ṗaıɓe Paʐʐṗuıc na ċoṁnuıɓe. Ɑᵹ ṗo ɓṗıaċṗa an
uᵹɒaıṗ. *Hoc autem tempore quædam classis Hibernica
vrædavit patriam in qua morabatur D. Patricius et con-
sueto Hibernorum more multi inde captivi ducti sunt,
inter quos erant D. Patricius ætatis anno* 16, *et duæ ejus
sorores Lupita et Darerca. Et ductus est D. Patricius in
Hiberniam captivus nono anno* Nıall *regis Hiberniæ, qui
potenter* 27. *annis regnavit, ac Britanniam et Angliam
usque ad mare quæ inter Angliam et Galliam est, vastavit.*
Ɒo ċuaıɓ (aṗ ṗe) ḟan am ṗo coɓlaċ Єıṗıonnaċ ɒo
ċṗeaċaɓ na cṗıċe ına ṗaıɓe an naoṁ Pḣaʐʐṗuıc, aᵹuṗ
maṗ ḟa ᵹıaċ le h-Єıṗıonnċaıɓ, ʐuᵹaɒaṗ ıomaɒ
bṗaıᵹɒe leó, aᵹuṗ an naoṁ Pḣaʐʐṗuıc maṗaon ṗıu
an aoıṗ ṗe m-blıaᵹaın ɒeuᵹ, aᵹuṗ ɓá ṗıaıṗ ɓo, maṗ
aʐa *Lupita et Darerca,* aᵹuṗ ʐuᵹaɓ naoṁ Pḣaɒṗuıc
na bṗaᵹaɓ an Єıṗınn an 9° blıaɓaın ɒo ḟlaıċıoṗ Neıll
Rıᵹ Єıṗınn, ɒo bı ᵹo neaṗʐṁaṗ 27 m-blıaᵹna ı ɓ-ḟlaı-
ċıoṗ Єıṗe, aᵹuṗ leṗ h-aıṗcceaɓ an ɓḣṗıoʐaın Saᵹṗaṗı
ᵹuṗ an ṁuıṗ aʐa ıoıṗ Saᵹṗoıɓ aᵹuṗ an Fṗaıncᵹe. Ɑṗ
na bṗıaċṗaṗa aṗ ınċṗeıɒċe ᵹo n-ɒeaċa Nıall naoı-
ᵹıallaċ ɒon ɓḣṗeaʐaın ṁoıṗ aᵹuṗ ᵹuṗ ᵹaɓ neaṗʐ
ınnʐe. Meaṗuım ḟoṗ ᵹuṗ ab ṗe lınn Neıll ɒo ɓeıċ
ḟan ɓḣṗeaʐaın ṁoıṗ aᵹ ᵹaɓáıl neıṗʐ, ɒo cuıṗ caɓlaċ
ɒ'aṗccoınn ımıoll na Fṗaıncce, ɒo'n ċṗıċ ṗe ṗaíoʐeaṗ
Armorica, ɒa n-ᵹoıṗċeaṗ anoıṗ an ɓḣṗeaʐaın ɓeuᵹ,
aᵹuṗ ᵹuṗ ab aıṗʐe ʐuᵹaɓ Paʐʐṗuıc cona ɓa ṗıaıṗ
a m-bṗoıɒ.

SECT. 7.—*Of the Invasion of Britain by the Picts and Scots.*

Αοιр Τιχεαρηα 393. Ιр ραη αмро οο βαοαη cιηηεαό Scuιτ αχυр ηα Ριcτι αχ αрccοιη αχυр αχ mιlleαό ηα όρεαταη moιρε, αχυр cuιрιο ηα όρεαċηα τεαċτα χο *Honorius* ιмрιр ο'ιαрραό cαβρα αιр, αχυр ηι όεαρηα αċτ рсрιοβαό ċuχċα οα ιαрραό ορρα α η-οιοċċιοll οο όεαηαṁ οοιβ рέιη, αχυр ċάιηιc όε рιη χο рαβαοαρ ηα όρεαċηα αιмрιр ιмċιαη οά. ειр рιη ρα leατрοm ηα Scoτ αχυр ηα b-Ριcτ, χιόεαό οα ειр рιη cuιрιο ηα όρεαċηα αрιр τεαċτα οοη Ρόιṁ, αχυр οο ηίο cαрάοιο τрuαιχαιχṁειl αр cрuαό οάιl ηο Scoτ αχυр ηα b-Ριcτ ορρα. Cuιрιο Ρόmαηαιχ leιχιοη οο рluαιχ αрmċα οα b-рuрταċτ, αχυр αр рοċταιη ηα όρεαταη οοιβ, τuχαοαρ ρειη αχυр ηα Scuιτ αχuρ ηα Ριcτι ιοmαο cοιmblιοcτ οα cειle; αχuρ αр m-beιτ τuιρρεαċ οο'η τ-рluαιχ Ρomαηαċ α οuβραοαρ рε όρεαċηα muр ηο clαό οο όεαηαṁ εατορρα ρειη αχuρ α η-ορος coṁαρроιη, αχuρ ηας ραιβε αр bрειċ οοιβ ρειη χuρ τιlleαό οο'η Ροιṁ. Ởαlα ηα m-όρεαċηαċ ιαρ η-ιṁτεαċτ ηα Ρόmαηαċ uαċα, τοχβuιο clαό рόο ο ṁuιρ χο muιρ ιοιр ιαο ρειη αχuρ ηα Scuιτ αχuρ ηα Ριcτ.

Αр ηα ċloр рιη οο cιηηεαό Scuιτ αχuр οο ηα Ριcτιβ χuρ ċрέιχεαοαρ ηα Ρόmαηαċα ηα όρεαċηα, lιηccιο ρειη ορρα αχuр bрιρτεαρ αη clαό, αχuр αιрιχċεαρ αη τιρ рιu χuρ b'eιχιη οο ηα όρεαċηα τεαċτα οο ċuιр αη τрεαр рεαċτ χο Ρόṁάηαċοιβ, οα ιαрραό ορρα χαη α leιχιοη οα ηάṁαιο βειċ αχ οεαηαṁ α luιτ χο οιβ-рεαрχαċ αṁuιl οο βαοαр. Ċειр рιη cuιριο ηα Ρόmάηαċα leιχεοη οιle οα b-рuрταċτ, αχuρ αр рοċταιη ηα όρεαταη οοιβ, τuχαοαρ ρειη αχuρ ηα Scuιτ αχuρ ηα Ριcτι ιοmαο cοιmbрlιοcτ οα ċειle, χuρ рuαχαοαρ ηα Ρόmαηαċα ταρ ċεορuιηη αη ċloό οο luαιόιοmαр

αμαċ ιαᴅ, αɣυρ αρ ƀ-ϝοιριȝċιn nα m-ᴆρεαċnαċ ᴅοιƀ
αṁlα ριn, α ᴅυƀραᴅαρ nα Roṁαnαċα nαċ ραιƀε ροċαρ
ᴅοιƀ ϝειn ċεαċċ ᴅά ƀ-ϝυρċαċċ αρ εαċċρα nι ρα mo,
αɣυρ α ϝέαċαιn cρευᴅ αn mοᴅ̇ nα ƀ-ϝευᴅϝαᴅαοιρ ιαᴅ
ϝειn ᴅο cυṁᴅαċ no ᴅο ᴅιon oρρα. Ωρ n-ιmċεαcċ
ιοmορρο ᴅο ρ̇lυαιȝ nα Roṁαnαιȝ υαċα ᴅο ċιοnρȝnαᴅαρ
αn cλοιᴅ̇ αċα o Muιρ ιᴅιρ Ωlbα αɣυρ ᴆρεαċοιn ᴅο
ᴅεαnαṁ ᴅ'οƀαιρ ċλοιċε, αɣυρ οċċ ċċροιȝċε nα ċιȝε,
αɣυρ ᴅα ċροιȝċε ᴅέαȝ ᴅαιρᴅε αnn, ᴅο ρειρ *Beda* ραn
cυιȝεαᴅ̇ cαιƀιοιl ᴅέαȝ ᴅο'n ċέυᴅ lεαƀαρ ᴅο ρċαιρ nα
Sαȝραn.

Mαρ ċύαlαᴅαρ nα Scυιċ αɣυρ nα Ριcċ ȝυρ ċυιρεαᴅαρ
nα Roṁαnαċα ορυιm ρε ċεαċċ ᴅ'ρ̇υρċαċċ nα m-ᴆρεαċnαċ αριρ, cυιριᴅ cρυιnιυȝαᴅ̇ αɣυρ cοιṁċιοnοl αρ ιοmαᴅ
ρ̇lυαιȝ αɣυρ ċυȝαιᴅ υċċ αρ αn cclαιᴅ̇ mυρριn ȝυρ
lιnȝεαᴅ̇ lεο ċαιριρ αɣυρ ȝο ċċυȝαᴅαρ nα ᴆρεαċαιn
υιlε, ιοnυρ ȝυρ ƀ'ειȝιn ᴅο ᴆρεαċnαċα α ccαċραċα
αɣυρ α nαρυρ ᴅο ċρέιȝεαn αɣυρ ᴅυl ᴅα n-ᴅιᴅεαn ϝέιn
ϝά ċοιllċεαᴅ̇ αɣυρ ρα ϝοραοιρεάċα ϝαρα conαċ bhίoᴅ̇
ᴅο ƀίαᴅ̇ αcα, αċċ ϝέοlṁαċ nα m-bεαċαᴅαċ n-αllċαᴅ̇
ᴅο nίċι ᴅο ϝειlȝ lεο, αɣυρ αn ċιαρṁ ᴅο ṁαιρ ᴅο ᴆhριο-
ċάnυιƀ ᴅο ρȝριοᴅ̇αᴅαρ ȝο ċρυάιȝṁειl ȝο *Consul* ᴅο ƀί
ραn Róṁ ᴅάρ ƀ'αιnm *Boetius* αȝ ιαρρυιᴅ̇ ϝυρċαċċα
αιρ; αɣυρ ιρε α ᴅυƀραᴅαρ ȝο ραƀᴅαᴅαρ ϝειn α ccυṁ-
ȝαċ ιᴅιρ α nαṁυιᴅ αɣυρ αn ṁυιρ, οιρ αn ορεαm ᴅιοƀ
ᴅο ᴅεαραᴅ̇ αȝαιᴅ̇ αρ αn ṁυιρ αȝ ċειċεαᴅ̇ ρερ α nαṁυιᴅ
ᴅο bαιᴅ̇ċι ιαᴅ, αɣυρ αn ορεαm ᴅιοƀ ᴅο ċιllεαᴅ̇ o'n
mυιρ ᴅο mαρƀċαόι lειρ α nαṁυιᴅ, αṁυιl α ᴅειρ *Beda*
ραn ċρεαρ cαιƀιοιl ᴅέαȝ ᴅο'n ċεαᴅ lεαƀαρ ᴅο ρċαιρ
nα Sαȝραn, αȝ αιċρ̇ριοċαl ƀριαċρα nα m-ᴆρεαċnαċ
αȝ εαȝnαċ ρε Roṁαnαċα αρ ϝοιρnεαρċ nα Scoċ αɣυρ
nα b-Ριcċ ορρα; αȝ ρο nα ƀριαċρα; *Repellunt barbari
ad mare, repellit mare ad barbaros. Inter hæc oriuntur*

duo genera funerum ; aut jugulamur aut mergimur.
Ruaıȝaıo na baꝓbaꝓéa ȝuꝓ an muıꝓ (aꝓ ꝓıao, aȝ laḃaıꝑc aꝓ na Scoca aȝuꝓ aꝓ na Pıccı) cıllıó an muıꝓ
aꝓ na baꝓbaꝓéa ınn ; ıoıꝓ an oa ċınneal ḃáıꝓ ꝓo
maꝓḃéaꝓ no baıoéeaꝓ ꝓınn (aꝓ ꝓıao); aꝓ ꝓo aꝓ ıoncuıcée ȝuꝓ ab moꝓ an ꝓoıꝓneaꝓc oo ḃı aȝ Scoca na
h-Єıꝓe aꝓ óꝓeaénaéa. Ɑ oeıꝓ *Nennius* ꝓeanuȝoaꝓ
óꝓeaénaé oo ꝓeıꝓ éꝓoınıc *Speed* ȝo ꝓaıbe leaécꝓom
aȝ Scocuıḃ aȝuꝓ aȝ Pıccıḃ aꝓ óhꝓıoéánuıḃ le ꝓe óa
ꝓééıc blıaȝaın, aȝuꝓ a oeıꝓ *Cambden* aȝ ceaéc leıꝓ
ꝓo, *Anno Domini* 500 *a Cæsaris ingressu Britannia
Pictorum et Scotorum immanitati relinquitur.* Ɖo ꝓaȝ-
baó ı cceann 500 blıaȝaın a n-oıaıó *Cæsar* oo ceaéc
o'n óhꝓıocaın ꝓa anıoéc na Scoc aȝuꝓ na b-Pıcc;
aȝuꝓ aꝓ ıoncuıcée ꝓın aꝓ bꝓıaꝓéa *Beda* ı 14 caıb.
oon leaḃaꝓ éeaona, maꝓ a n-abaıꝓ, aȝ laḃaıꝑc aꝓ
Єıꝓıonnéaıḃ, *Revertuntur impudentes grassatores Hiberni
domum post non longum tempus reversuri.* Cıllıo (aꝓ
ꝓe) aıꝓȝéeoıꝓe aınıuoe Єıꝓıonnaéa oá ccıȝ aꝓ cı
cıllceaó ȝo ȝꝓoo caꝓ anaıꝓ ; aꝓ na bꝓıaéꝓaıḃꝓı *Beda*
aꝓ ıoncuıcée ȝo ccuȝoaoıꝓ Єıꝓeanna ꝓuaıȝ ȝo mınıc
oaꝓccoın na óꝓıocáıne. Ɖala na m-óꝓeaénaé oa
eıꝓ ꝓın, oo ḃaoaꝓ aımꝓıꝓ ıméıan oa noıꝓleaé aȝuꝓ oa
n-aꝓccoın aȝ Scocoıḃ aȝuꝓ aȝ Pıccı, ıaꝓ na ccꝓeıȝean
na Roṁanaéa.

SECT. 8.—*That Scotia was anciently the Name of Ireland.*

Iꝓ ıomóa uȝoaıꝓ aȝa ꝓuıóıuȝaó ȝuꝓ ab o *Scotia* ꝓa
h-aınm o'Єıꝓe, aȝuꝓ ȝuꝓ ab o'Єıꝓıonéaıḃ oo ȝoıꝓéı
cınneaó Scuıc.
Ɑca *Beda* ꝓan ééao éaıbıoıl oo'n ééao leaḃaꝓ oo ꝓcaıꝓ
na Saȝꝓan aȝa ꝓaóa ȝuꝓ ab ı Єıꝓe oúéaó oılıoꝓ na

Scoꞇ. Aᵹ ꞃo maꞃ a ꝺeıꞃ ; *Hibernia proprie Scotorum patria est.* Aꞃ ı Єıꞃe ꝺuꞇaꝺ óıleaꞃ na Scoꞇ. A ꝺeıꞃ an ꞇ-uᵹꝺaꞃ ceaꝺna, aᵹ ꞃꞓꞃıoꝺaꝺ aꞃ na naoṁaıꞑ, nıꝺ ꞇıᵹ leıꞃ an nıꝺ ceaꝺna ; *Sanctus Cilianus et duo socii ejus ab Hibernia Scotorum insula venerant.* A h-Єıꞃeann oılean na Scoꞇ, (aꞃ ꞃe,) ꞇaınıc *Cilianus* naoṁꞇa aᵹuꞃ a ꝺa ċoṁꞇaċ. Aꞃ ꞃo ıꞃ ıonꞇuıcꞇe ᵹo ꞇꞇuᵹꞇaoí cınneaꝺ Scuıꞇ aꞃ Єıꞃıonċaıꞑ ꞃé lın *Beda*, ꝺo ṁaıꞃ a ccean ꞃeaċꞇ ccéaꝺ blıaᵹaın ꝺeıꞃ CRIOSꝹ.

Aᵹ ꞃo maꞃ a ꝺeıꞃ *Jonas* Aꞑꞑ aᵹ laꝺaıꞃꞇ aꞃ Colman ꞃan ċéaꝺ caıꞑıꝺıl, *Columbanus, qui et Columba vocatur, in Hibernia ortus est : eam Scotorum gens incolit.* Colman (aꞃ ꞃe) ꞃe ꞃáıꝺꞇeaꞃ Columb, an Єıꞃe a ꞃuᵹaꝺ é, maꞃ a n-áıꞇıᵹıꝺ cıneaꝺ Scuıꞇ. Cıᵹ ꞃoꞃ *Origius* ꝺo ṁaıꞃ leıꞇ aꞃꞇıᵹ ꝺo ceıꞇꞃe ċéaꝺ blıaᵹaın ꝺo CRIOSꝹ, leıꞃ an nıꝺ ceaꝺna. Aᵹ ꞃo maꞃ a ꝺeıꞃ ꞃan ꝺaꞃa caıꞑıꝺıl ꝺo'n ċeaꝺ leaꝺaꞃ, *Hibernia Scotorum gentibus colitur.* Aꞃıaꝺ cınneaꝺ no Scoꞇ áıꞇıᵹeaꞃ Єıꞃe. Aꞃ ꞃolluꞃ ᵹo cıoꞇċıon ᵹo ꞇꞇuᵹꞇáoı leıꞃ na h-uᵹꝺaıꞃꞃı *Scotia* uıꞃꞃı.

Aᵹ ꞃo maꞃ a ꝺeıꞃ *Cæsarius* aᵹ ꞃꞓꞃıoꝺaꝺ aꞃ Cılıan naoṁꞇa ; *Beatus Cilianus Scotorum genere ;* Cılıan naoṁꞇa ꝺo cınneaꝺ na Scoꞇ ; aᵹuꞃ a ꝺeıꞃ ᵹo ᵹꞃoꝺ ꝺá éıꞃ na ꞑꞃıaꞇꞃaꞃa, *Scotia quæ et Hibernia dicitur.* Aꞃ ꞃo aꞃ ıonꞇuıcꞇe ᵹuꞃ aꞑ aınm ꝺ'Єıꞃeann ꝺo ꞃıoꞃ *Scotia* aṁuıl aꞃeaꝺ *Hibernia.*

Cuıᵹꞇeaꞃ ꞃıꞃınne an neıꞇeꞃı a ꞑꞃıaꞃꞇa *Capgravius* aᵹ ꞃᵹꞃıoꝺaꝺ aꞃ Columb náoṁꞇa ; aᵹ ꞃo maꞃ a ꝺeıꞃ, *Hibernia enim antiquitus Scotia dicta est, de qua gens Scotorum Albaniam Britanniæ majori proximam, quæ ab eventu modo Scotia dicitur, inhabitans, originem duxit et progressum habuit.* Ꝺo ᵹoıꞃꞇı analloꝺ *Scotia* ꝺ'eıꞃınn ó ꞑ-ꞃuıl cınneaꝺ Scuıꞇ aꞇá aᵹ áıꞇıuᵹaꝺ na h-Alꞑan αρ ροιȝρι ɒο'n ბhριοȼάιn αρ mo, αȝυρ ȝαιρȼεαρ ɒο'r Cllbαιn *Scotia* αnοιρȝo ȼεαȝṁυιρεαȼ ó Θιριnn ό ᖯ-ρυιl α m-bυnαᖫυρ αȝυρ α n-ɒαιl.

Cιȝ *Marianus Scotus* υȝɒαρ Cllbαnαȼ lειρ ρο, αȝ ρϲριο- ბαᖫ αιρ *Cilian* nαοṁȼα, mαρ α n-αbαιρ; *Eliamsi hodie Scotia proprie vocetur ea Britanniæ pars quæ ipsi Angliæ continens ad Septentrionem vergit, olim tamen eo nomine Hiberniam notatam fuisse ostendit V. Beda, cum e Scythia Pictorum gentem in Hiberniam venisse ait, ibique Scotorum gentem invenisse.* Cαρ ϲεαnn ȝo ȼȼυȝαɒαρ ȝo ɒιlιορ *Scotia* ɒ' αιnm αρ αn ϲϲυιɒ υɒ ɒο'n ბhριοȼάιn αȼα ɒο'r lειȼ ȼυαιᖫ ɒo Shαȝροιᖯ ȼάιȼε ρια, mαιρεαᖫ ροιllριȝιᖫ *Beda* ȝo n-ȝοιρȼι αn ȼ-αιnm ριn ɒ'Θιριnn αnαllοɒ, οιρ αn ȼαn α ɒειρ ϲιnnεαᖫ nα b-Ριϲȼ ɒo ȼεαȼȼ o'n *Scythia* ι n-Θιριnn, α ɒειρ ȝυρ αb ιαɒ ϲιnnεαᖫ nα Sϲοȼ ρυαρα- ɒαρ ρompα ιnnȼε, αȝυρ ɒo ᖯριȝ ȝυρ αb ό ϲιnnεαᖫ nα Sϲοȼ ɒo ρlοιnnεαᖫ αn ϲρίοȼ, αρ *Scotia* ρα h-αιnm ᖫι αn ȼαn ροιn.

Cllρ ιοnȼυιϲȼε α ᖯριαρȼαιᖯ *Cæsarius* ɒo ṁαιρ ɒο'n lειȼ αρȼιȝ ɒo ϲύιȝ ϲεαɒ blιαȝαιn ɒo CRIOSƆ ȝυρ *Scotia* ρα h-αιnm ɒ'Θιριnn; αȝ ρο mαρ α ɒειρ: *Qui de purgatorio dubitat, Scotiam pergat, Purgatorium S. Patricii intret, et de purgatorii pœnis amplius non dubitabit,* Ɔι be ϲυιρεαρ ϲοnȼαᖯαιρȼ ι b-Ρυρȝαɒοιρ, ȼριαllαɒ ȝo *Scotia,* ειρȝε ι ρȼεαȼ ι b-ρυρȝαɒοιρ nαοṁ Ραȼȼρυιϲ, αȝυρ nι ϲυιρρα ϲοnȼαᖯαιρȼ α b-ριαnαᖫ ρυρȝαɒορα o ροιn αmαȼ. Cl ᖯριαȼροιᖯ αn υȝɒαιρρι αρ ιοnȼυιϲȼε ȝυρ αb αιnm ϲοιȼϲιοnn ɒ'Θιριnn ρα'n αm ροιn *Scotia,* οιρ nι ᖯ-ρυιl αοnαιȼ ι n-Cllboιn ɒα n-ȝοιρȼεαρ Ρυρȝα- ɒοιρ Ρhαȼȼρυιϲ, αȝυρ ιρ ρollυρ ȝυρ αb ι n-Θιριnn αȼα αn άιȼ ɒ'α n-ȝοιρȼεαρ ι.

Cιȝ *Cæsarius* lειρ αn nιɒ ϲεαɒnα αȝ ρȝριοᖯαᖫ αρ *Boni- facius* nαοṁȼα mαρ α n-αbαιρ, *Hibernia Scotiæ sibi*

K

nomen etiam vindicabat : quia tamen ex Hibernia ista Scotorum pars quædam egressa est, in eaque Britanniæ arva quæ Picti jam habebant, consederunt, ii quidem principio a duce suo Reuda Dalreudini dicti fuerunt, ut ait V. Beda. Postea tamen Pictos inde ipsos exegerunt, et Boreale totum illud latus obtinuerunt ; eique vetus gentis suæ nomen indiderunt ; ita ut Scotorum gens una fuerit, sed Scotia duplex facta sit, una vetus et propria in Hibernia, recentior altera in Septentrionali Britannia.

Do bi pop *Scotia* o'ainm ap Eininn ; ʒioeao ceana oo bpiʒ ʒo ccainic o'n Eininn ceaona opoinʒ o'aipiʒte ʒo hoipeap na opiotaine map an aiciʒeaoap na Picci, oo puioeaoap map aon piu an opeampo ceana ap ccup o na ccaoipeac pein Reuoa, .i. Caipbpe Rioʒpooa, a oeipteap *Dalreudini* .i. Oailpiaoa piu, amuil a oeip *Beda;* ʒioeao oo puaʒaoap oa eip pin na Picci pein, aʒup oo ʒabaoap an leit tuaio oo'n cpic pin uile aʒup tuʒaoap peanainm a ccpice pein uippi, ionup ʒup ab aoncinneao amain Scot atá ann ; ʒioeao ata oa *Scotia* ann ; a h-aon oiob appuio oileap; aʒup an oapa *Scotia* ata nuaio ipin leait tuaio oo'n opiotáin. Do beipim tpi neite oo'm aipe a bpiatpoib an uʒoaip po. An ceao ní oiob, ʒup ab iao na h-Eipionnaiʒ ʒo pipinneac na Scuit. An oapa ni, ʒup ab oo Ohailpiaoa oo ʒaipmteap Scuit i n-Alboin ap tup, oo bpiʒ ʒup ab iao oo pine ʒabaltup ap na Picci ap tup i pin cpic pin. An tpeap ni, map a oeip ʒup ab i Eipe *Scotia* oilior pean, aʒup ʒup ab i Alba *Scotia* nuao, aʒup ʒup ab iao Scuit oo ʒaipteap *Scotia* aip ttup oi.

A oeip *Buchananus* uʒoap Albanac, aʒ teact leip an nio cceaona pan 34. leatanao pan oapa leabap oo Staip na h-Alba, map a n-abaip ; *Principio cum utrique, id est Hiberniæ incolæ, et coloni eorum in Albaniam missi,*

Scoti appellarentur, ut discrimine aliquo alteri ab alteris distinguerentur, ab initio cœpere alteri Scoti Hiberni, alteri Scoti Albini vocari. Do ḃríġ (ar sé), go n-goirṫí ar tús Scuit d'aiṫiġṫeoiriḃ na h-Eireann, agus don ḟoirinne do ċuaiḋ uaṫa d'áitiúġaḋ na h-Alban, ionnus le h-eidirdealuġaḋ eigin, go m-biaiḋ deifir eatorra leaṫ ar leiṫ do ṫionsgnadar ó ṫús Scoit Eirionda do gairm do ḋruing ḋíoḃ, agus Scoit Alba do'n ḟoirinn oile. Ar na briaṫruiḃsi *Buchananus*, tuigṫear ḋá ní: an cead ní, gur ab a h-Eirinn do ċuaiḋ Scuit d'áitiuġaḋ na h-Alban; agus an dara níḋ, gur gnaṫ ainm d'Eirionncaiḃ Scuit ó ṫús.

Sect. 9.—*Testimonies of some English Writers concerning the national Character of the Irish People.*

Ag so an teist do beir Maiġistir Gúd, sagart Sagsonaċ (do ḃí ag seolaḋ scoile i Luimneaċ), ar Eirionnċuiḃ, an tan fa h-aois do'n Tiġearna 1566 bliaḋna: "Cinneaḋ so (ar sé), ata laidir i g-corp, agus ata luṫṁar, aga m-bí inntinn ḟoirtil ard, intleaċt géur ḃios cogaṁuil, neaṁċoigealtaċ air a m-beaṫaiḋ, ag a m-bí fulang saoṫair, fuaċta agus ocrais, ag a m-bí claonaḋ re déanaṁ drúise, ḃios roiċeannsa re h-áoiḋeaḋuiḃ, buainḟearṁaċ i n-gráḋ, doḟáraiġṫe i ḃ-faltanas, ḃíos soiċreideaṁnaċ, ḃíos fonnṁar ar ċlu d'ḟaġail, bíos neaṁḟoiġideaċ ar ṁasla, no air éagcóir d'fulang."

Ag so fos an teist do ḃeir *Stanihurst* orra, eaḋon, "dream ro ḟuilingṫioċ air saoṫarṫoiḃ tar an uile ċinéil do ḋaoiniḃ, agus is annaṁ ḃíos tláiṫ i n-guasaċtaiḃ."

A deir *Spencer* gur ab ó Eirionnċuiḃ fuaradar na

Saṡronaiṫ aibṁiceap aip ccup, aṡup ba peip pin, ni
paib piop liceapoacca ap biṫ aṡ na Saṡronaiṫib ṡo
b-puapaoap ó Eipionnċuib í.

Ap pollup [a oeip *Keating*] ṡup ab o'anplaiṫiop aṡup
o'éaccóip, aṡup oo neaṁċoiṁeao ap a n-oliṫeao peín
aṡ uaċcapanaib Ṡall a n-Eipinn ṫáinic iomao eap-
úṁla na n-ṡaóioiol oo pmaċc ṡall, oip ni ṁeapuim
ṡo b-puil cinneao' pan Eopaip ap mo oo biaio uṁal
oo oliṫeao inaio Eipioná, oa poinnci coṁépom na
oliṫeao piu: aṡup ap í po ceipc oo beip Seón *Davis*
(pan leaċanaċ oeuṡeanaċ oo'n ċeao leabap oo pcpíob
ap Eipino) oppa ; aṡ pó map a oeip : " Ni b-puil
cinneao pa'n nṡpéin len' ab annpa ceapc aṡup coṁépom bpeaiċeaṁnup ni ap peapp inaio Eipionoa, aṡup
ap mo biao papuiṫċe ina iao lé na ċup a n-ṡnioṁ,
bioo ṡup ab na naṫaio pein oo paċao, aċc ṡo b-pa-
ṡuio oion aṡup poċap na oliṫeao an c-an iappuio e aip
ċuip coṁépom."

CHAPTER VI.

SACRED LESSONS—CONSISTING OF PASSAGES EXTRACTED FROM THE IRISH VERSION OF THE HOLY SCRIPTURES.

SECT. 1.—*From the Proverbs of Solomon.*

Seannṗáiŏꞇe Sholaiṁ ṁic Ďhaiḃi piꝺ Iꝛꞃáel.

1. Aꞇa ꝛlíꝺe ann ꝺo ċiꞇeaꝶ ꝺíꝶeaċ ꝺo ŏuine, aċꞇ iꝛ é a ċꝛíoċ ꝛin ꝛlíꝺꞇeaċa an ḃáiꝶ.

2. An ꞇe ꝶáꝶuiꝺioꝶ an ḃoċꞇ maꝶluiꝺiŏ ꝶe a Chꝶuꞇaiꝺꞇeoiꝶ ; aċꞇ an ꞇe onóꝶuiꝺioꝶ e ḃi ꞇꝶócaiꝶe ann ꝺo'n ḃoċꞇ.

3. Iompoiꝺiŏ ꝶꝶeaꝺꝶa ṁacánꞇa ꝶeaꝶꝺ : aċꞇ ḃꝶoꝶꞇuiꝺiŏ ḃꝶiaꞇꝶa ḃoꝶḃa an ꝶeaꝶꝺ.

4. Aꞇáiꝺ ꝛúile an ꞇIꝒhEARNA ann ꝺaċ uile ḃall, aꝺ ꝶeuċuin aiꝶ an olc aꝺuꝛ aiꝶ an maiꞇ.

5. Ďo ꝺní cꝶóiŏe ꝶuꝺaċ ꝺnúiꝶ ꝶuilḃiꝶ : aċꞇ le ꝺóḃꝶón an ċꝶóiŏe ḃꝶiꝶꞇeaꝶ an ꝛpioꝶaꝺ.

6. Ď'ꝶeaꝶꝶ beaꝺán maille ꝶe h-eaꝺla an ꞇIꝒhEARNA, ná ionnmuꝛ móꝶ aꝺuꝛ buaiŏꝶeaŏ maille ꝶiꝶ.

7. Iꝛ ꝶeaꝶꝶ ꝺinneiꝶ luiḃionn maꝶ a m-bi ꝺꝶaŏ, na ꝺaṁ biaŏꞇa aꝺuꝛ ꝶuaꞇ maille ꝶiꝶ.

8. Ďi ꝛlíꝺe an amaꝺáin ꝺíꝶeaċ ionna ꝶúiliḃ ꝶéin : aċꞇ iꝛ cꝶíonna an ꞇé éiꝶꞇioꝶ ꝶe cóṁaiꝶle.

9. Iꝛ ꝶaꝺa an ꞇIꝒhEARNA ó'n ccionnꞇaċ : aċꞇ ꝺo ċluin ꝛé ꝺuíŏe an ꝶíꝶéin.

10. An ꞇé ŏuilꞇaꝶ múnaŏ ꞇaꝶcuiꝶniꝺiŏ ꝶé a anam ꝶéin : aċꞇ an ꞇé úṁluiꝺioꝶ ꝺo ꝛmaċꞇ, ꝺo ꝺeiḃ ꝶé ꞇuiꝝꝶi.

K 2

11. Iṗ é eaʒla an TIƷheARHA ceaʒaṗʒ na h-eaʒna; aʒuṗ acá úṁlacc ṗoıṁe onóıṗ.

12. An uaıṗ caıċnıo ṗlıʒ́ce an ouıne leıṗ an o-TI-ƷheARHA oo ḃeıṗ ṗé aıṗ a náṁuıo ṗeın ḃeıċ ṗíoóac ṗıṗ.

13. Ca ṁéao ıṗ ṗeáṗṗ eaʒna o'ṗaʒáıl ná óṗ? aʒuṗ cuıʒṗı o'ṗaʒáıl ıṗ cóṗa í oo ċoʒa ná aıṗʒıoo.

14. Iṗ mó ċéıo aċṁuṗán a ṗceaċ an ouıne ċṗíonna, na céao buılle ann amaoán.

15. An c-amaoan ṗéın, an uaıṗ ḃíoṗ ṗé 'na ċoċo, meaṗcaṗ cṗíonna é; aʒuṗ an cé óṗuıoıoṗ a ḃeal, bı ṗe meaṗca 'na ouıne ċuıʒṗıonaċ.

16. Ʒıò ḃe ṗṗeaʒṗaṗ cúıṗ ṗoıṁe a cloṗ, ıṗ amaoánaċc aʒuṗ naıṗe oó é.

17. Ʒıò b'é ḃıoṗ aṗ ccúṗ ıonna cúıṗ ṗeın, ṗaoılceaṗ cóıṗ oo ḃeıċ aıʒe; aċc cıʒ a ċóṁaṗṗa aʒuṗ ṗṗíonuıò ṗé é.

18. An cé aʒa m-bí cṗuaıʒe oo'n ḃoċc áıṗlıʒıò ṗe oo'n TIƷheARHA; aʒuṗ aṗ an nıò oo ḃéaṗa ṗe uaò ıocṗuıò ṗé ṗıṗ é aṗíṗ

19. Ʒıò b'é óúnuṗ a ċluaṗa ṗe h-éıʒıoṁ na m-boċc, cóṁaıṗcṗıo ṗé ṗeın maṗ an ʒ-ceaona, aċc ní cluınṗıʒ́ceaṗ é.

20. Ceaʒaıṗʒ an leanḃ ṗan c-ṗlıʒ́e annı aṗ cóıṗ oo ımċeaċo: aʒuṗ an c-an bıaṗ ṗé aoṗca nı ċṗéıʒṗıò ṗé í.

21. Óí leıṁe ceanʒaılce a ccṗóıóe leınḃ; aċc cuıṗ-ṗıò ṗlac an ṗmaċcuıʒ́ce a ḃ-ṗao uaò í.

22. An ḃ-ṗaıcıonn cú ouıne oíċċıollaċ ıonna ʒnoċuı-ʒıḃ? ṗeaṗṗuıò ṗe a láċaıṗ ṗíoʒ; ní a láċaıṗ óaoıne uıṗíṗıol ṗeaṗṗaṗ ṗe.

27. Ʒleuṗ ċ'obaıṗ amúıʒ́, aʒuṗ oean oıṗeaṁnaċ óuıc ṗéın í annṗa ṁaċaıṗe; aʒuṗ 'na óıaıò ṗın oéan oo ċíʒ́.

28. Ná luaċʒáıṗıʒ́ an uaıṗ ċuıcṗıoṗ oo náṁaıo, aʒuṗ ná ʒáıṗoıʒeaò oo ċṗoíóe an uaıṗ oo ʒeıḃ ṗe cuıṗleaò.

29. Αn b-ρaιcιonn τú ouιne cρíonna ιona baραṁuιl
ρéιn? ιρ mó an oóιȝ ιρ cóιρ oo beιċ aρ amaoán na aρ.

30. Na maoιò ċú ρeιn aρ an la a máραċ; óιρ ní
ρéιoιρ τú cρéao oo beaρρaò lá leιρ.

31. Iρ oíleaρ cneaòa na cáραιo; aċτ ιρ cealȝaċ póȝa
na naṁaιo.

32. Ȝéαρuιò ιαρραnn ιαρραnn oιle; maρροιn ȝéaρuι-
ȝιoρ ouιne ȝnúιρ a cáραo.

33. Ófò an ouιne ραιòbιρ cρíonna ιonna ċuιȝριn ρéιn;
aċτ ρcρúouιȝ an boċτ aȝa m-bι τuιȝρι amaċ é.

34. Ȝιò b'é cειlιoρ a ρeacuιòe, ní bιa bιρeaċ αιρ; aċτ
ȝι b'é aoṁaρ aȝuρ ċρéιȝιoρ ιao, oo ȝeaòρa ρé τρócaιρe.

35. Oo beιρ eaȝla an ouιne ράιnτéuρ lé: aċτ an τe
ċuιριoρ ooċċuρ annρa o-ΤΙȜhΕΑRΝΑ bιαιò ρé oaιn-
ȝιon.

II.—*St. Matthew*, ch. xviii. vv. 21–35.

21. Αρ n-oul oo Ρheaoaρ 'na ιonnραιò an τραċ ριn, a
ouòaιρτ ρé, Α ΤhΙȜhΕΑRΝΑ ȝa a mιoncaċo oó
òéana mo òeaρbράċaιρ coιρ a m'aȝaιò, aȝuρ maιċρeaρ
mé òo? an ȝo nuιȝe ρeaċoṁaò h-uaιρ?

22. Α oeιρ Ιoρa ριρ, Νι abρuιm ριoτ, Ȝuρ an ρeaċoṁaò h-uaιρ aṁaιn: aċo, Ȝo ροιċe an ρeaċoṁoȝao ρeaċo
nuaιρe.

23. Αρ an áoòaρροιn ιρ coρṁuιl ρíoȝaċo neiṁe ρé
ρíȝ áιριȝċe, le'ρ b'áιll cúnτaρ oo òéanaò ρé na ρeaρb-
ρóȝanτuιòιb.

24. Αȝuρ an τραċ oo τιonnρȝaιn ρé cúnταρ oo òéanaò, τuȝaò ċuιȝe neaċ, o'aρ òlíȝ ρé oειċ míle τalann.

25. Αȝuρ an ταn náρ b'éιoιρ leιρ na ριaċaρo o'íoc,
oo aιċιn a ċιȝeaρna é ρéιn, aȝuρ a bean, aȝuρ a clan,
aȝuρ a ραιò aιȝe, oo ρειc, oo ċum na b-ριac oo òíol.

26. Ar an áḋḃarrsoin ag déanaḋ úṁla do'n t-searḃ-foġantuiġe sin, do iarr sé aṫċuinġiḋ air, ag raḋ, A ṫiġearna, déana fóiġid riom, agus do ḃéara me an t-iomlán ḋuit.

27. Ann sin ar n-gaḃáil truaiġe móire tíġearna ann oglaoic úd, do léig se uaḋ e, agus do ṁaiṫ sé na fiaċa ḋó.

28. Agus ag dul amaċ do'n t-searḃfoġantuiġ úd, fuair se aon d'a ċóiṁṡearḃfóġantuiḋiḃ féin, d'ar ḋlíġ sé cead píġinn: agus ar na ḟosdaḋ, rug sé air scornuiġ air, ag ráḋ, díol rium an niḋ ḋlíġeas tú.

29. Agus ag tuitim d'á ċóiṁṡearḃfoġantuiḋ ag a ċosuiḃsean, do ġuíḋ sé é, ag ráḋ, dean fóiġid riom, agus do ḃéarfa me an t-iomlán ḋuit.

30. Aċd nior ḃ'áill leisean sin: aċd ar n-imṫeaċd ḋó do ṫeilg se a b-prísún e, no go n-íocad se na fiaċa.

31. Agus an traṫ do ċonncadar a ċóiṁṡearḃfóġan-tuiḋerion na néiṫe do rinneaḋ, do ġaḃ doilġeas róṁór iad, agus tangadar, agus do ḟoillsiġeadar d'á d-tíġ-earna ġaċ níḋ dá n-dearnaḋ ann.

32. Annsoin do ċuir a ṫiġearna fios airsean, agus a deir sé ris, A ḋroiċṡearḃfóġantuiḋ, do ṁaiṫ mé na fiaċa úd uile ḋuit, do ḃríġ gur ċuir tú impiḋe oram:

33. Agus a né nár ċóir ḋuitsi trócaire do ḋéanaḋ ar do ċóiṁṡearḃfoġantuiḋ féin, aṁail agus mar do rinne mise trócaire ortsa ?

34. Agus an n-gaḃáil feirge a ṫiġearna, ṫug se do na céasadóiriḃ e, go n-íocaḋ se a ḟiaċa uile ris.

35. Agus is mar sin do ḋéana m'Aṫair neaṁḋasa ribsi, muna ṁaiṫfe gaċ aonduine agaiḃ a ḋearḃráṫair ó ḃur g-croiḋṫiḃ a g-cionnta.

III.—*Romans*, ch. xii. and xiii.

Chap. xii.

1. Αιρ αn άόϬαppoιn ρίριm ɒ'αἐἑuιnʒe οραιϬ, α όeαρϬράιἑρεαἑα, ἑρé ἑρόϲαιρε Ɗé, Ϭuρ ʒ-cuιρρ ɒο ἑαϬαιρϲ 'nα ϬεοιοόϬαιρϲ, nαοmἑα ʒeαnαmαιl ɒο Ɗhια, Ϭuρ ρeιρϬιρ ρεαρúnϲα.

2. Αʒuρ nα cumαιό ριϬ ϝéιn ριρ αn ϲ-ραοʒαλρα; αἑϲ cuιριό ριϬ ϝeιn αιἑeαρραἑ cροἑα ρε hαἑnuαόuʒαό Ϭuρ nιnnϲιnne, ιοnnuρ ʒο m-bιαό α όeρϬ αʒuιϬ cρeαɒ í ϲοιl mαιϲ, ʒeαnαmuιl, ɒιοnʒmαlα Ɗé.

3. Οιρ α ɒeιριm ρe ʒαἑ αοn εαορuιϬρe, ϲρeρ αn nʒράʒ ɒο ἑuʒαό όαm [ʒαn ʒαϬαιl ρe α άιρ] ní ɒο ἑuιʒρ'ιn ορ cιοn αn neιἑe ιρ ιοmἑuϬαιό όο ɒο ἑuιʒριn: αἑϲ α ϲuιʒρι ɒο Ϭeιἑ ɒο ρeιρ mεαραρρόαἑɒα αmαιl αρ ɒο ροιnn Ɗια ρe ʒαἑ αοιnneαἑ míορuρ ἑρeιοιm.

4. Οιρ ɒο ρeιρ mαρ αϲα ιοmαɒ ball αʒuιnn α néαnἑόρρ αmαιn, αʒuρ nαἑ eαnοιϝιʒ αmαιn αϲά αʒ ná huιle ϬαllαιϬ ριn:

5. Αρ mαρ αn ʒ-céαɒnα, αϲαmαοιοne móραn αρ neαnἑορρ α ʒ-Cριορϲ, αʒuρ ʒαἑ αοn ϝο leιἑ αρ m-ballαιϬ αʒα ἑeιle.

6. Uιme ριn αιρ m-beιἑ ɒο ἑιοόlαιcιϬ euʒραmlα αʒuιn ɒο ρeιρ nα nʒραρ ἑuʒαό όúιnn, mάρ ϝάιόeαɒóιρeαἑό [αϲα αʒuιn, ɒeαnαm ϝαιόeαɒóιρeαἑό] ɒο ρéιρ meuɒ αn ἑρeιοιm;

7. Ηο mάρ οιϝιʒ [αϲα αʒuιnn, ϲuʒαm αιρe] ɒο'n οιϝιʒ: no αn ϲe ἑeαʒuιρʒeαρ, ϲuʒαό αιρe όα ἑeαʒuρʒ;

8. Ηο αn ϲe ɒο Ϭeιρ ϝοιρceαɒαl uαόα [ϲuʒαό αιρe] όα ϝοιρceαɒαl: αn ϲe ροιnneαρ [αnɒeιρϲ, ροιneαό] í mαιlle ρe neαmuρcóιɒ; αnϲé αʒά Ϭ-ϝuιl ceαnuρ [όρ cιοnn ἑαιἑ, ɒeαnαό e] mαιlle ρe όúἑραἑɒ; αn ϲe ɒο ʒní ϲρόcαιρe, [ɒeαnαό í] mαιlle ρe ρúϬαἑuρ.

9. ᴅɪοὸ ƀυη n-ᵹηάὸ ᵹαn ċеɪłᵹ. ᴅɪοὸ ᵹηάɪn αᵹαɪƀ αɪη αn οłс; [αᵹυη] сеαnᵹłυɪᵹ ᴅοn ṁαɪċ.

10. ᴅɪοὸ ᴚοɪł αᵹυɪƀ ὸ'α ċеɪłе mαɪłłе ηе ᵹηάὸ ƀηάɪċ-ηеαṁυɪł; αᵹ ᴚαƀαɪηᴚ οnόηα υαɪƀ ᵹαċ αοn αᵹ ᴅυł ηοɪṁе α ċеɪłе.

11. Nα [ƀίᵹɪὸ] łеɪηᵹеαṁυɪł α n-ᵹnοċυɪᵹɪƀ; [ƀɪᵹɪὸ] αɪη ꜰɪυċαὸ αn ƀυη ᵹηɪοηαɪο; αᵹ ᴅеαnαὸ ηеɪηƀίηɪ ᴅο'n ꜱɪᵹеαηnα.

12. Αᵹ ᴅеαnαὸ ᵹαɪηᴅеċαɪη ᴚηέ ὸόċċαη; ꜰοɪᵹɪᴅеαċ α m-ƀυαɪὸеαηċυɪƀ сόṁnυɪᵹеαċ α n-υηnαɪᵹе.

13. Αᵹ сόṁηοɪn ηɪη nα nαοṁαɪƀ ɪοnnα ηɪαċᴅαnυηαɪƀ; αᵹ ᵹηάὸυᵹαὸ łυсὸ αοɪὸеαċᴅα ᴅο ᵹłαсαὸ.

14. ꜱαƀηυɪὸ ƀυη m-ƀеαnnαċὸ ᴅο'n ᴅηеɪm ὸɪƀηеη ηɪƀ: ᴚαƀηυɪὸ ƀυη m-ƀеαnnαċὸ [ᴅοɪƀ], αᵹυη nα mαłłυɪὸе[ɪαὸ].

15. ᴅɪοὸ ᵹαɪηᴅеαċυη οηαɪƀ mαηαοn ηɪη αn mυɪnnᴚɪη αɪη α ƀꜰυɪł ᵹαɪηᴅеαċυη, αᵹυη ƀɪᵹɪὸ αᵹ сαοɪ mαηαοn ηɪη αn mυɪnnᴚɪη ᴅο ᵹnί сαοɪ.

16. Ᵹο mαὸ hαοnᴚοɪł ὸɪƀ ηе ċеɪłе. Nα [ƀɪᵹɪὸ] αɪηὸɪnn-ᴚɪnеαċ αċὸ сυmαɪὸ ηɪƀ ꜰеɪn ηɪη αn n-ᴅηеɪm ɪη ίηłе. Nα ƀɪᵹɪὸ ᵹłɪс αnn ƀυη m-ƀαηαṁłυɪƀ ꜰеɪn.

17. Nα ᴅέαnαɪὸ οłс α nαᵹαɪὸ υɪłс αɪη еɪnnеαċ. ᴅɪοὸ сύηαm nα nеɪċеαnn mαɪċ οηαɪƀ α ƀ-ꜰɪαὸnυɪηе nα n-υɪłе ὸαοɪnе.

18. Mαη ꜰеɪοɪη έ, αn ṁеɪο ċɪᵹ ὸɪƀηе ὸе, ƀɪοὸ ηɪοċċαɪn αᵹαɪƀ ηɪη nα h-υɪłе ὸαοɪnɪƀ.

19. Α ċάɪηᴅе ᵹηάὸαċα, nα ᴅέαnαɪὸ ᴅɪοᵹαłᴚυη αɪη ƀυη ηοn ꜰеɪn, αċὸ ꜰαnαɪὸ ηɪη αn ƀ-ꜰеɪηᵹ: όɪη αᴚά ηᵹηɪοƀċα[ɪη] łеαmηα αn ᴅɪοᵹαłᴚυη; ᴅο ƀеαηꜰα mе сυɪᴚɪυᵹαὸ [υαɪm] α ᴅеɪη αn ꜱɪᵹеαηnα.

20. Uɪmе ηɪn ᴅα ηαɪƀ οсαηυη αɪη ᴅο nαṁυɪο, ᴚαƀαɪη ƀɪαὸ ὸό; ᴅα ηαɪƀ ᴚαηᴚ αɪη, ᴚαƀαɪη ᴅеοċ ὸο: όɪη ᴚηέ ηο ᴅο ὸέαnαὸ ὸυɪᴚ сαηηꜰυɪὸ ᴚυ ᵹηίοηαċ αɪη α ċеαnn.

21. Nα ƀеɪηеαὸ αn ᴚ-οłс ƀυαɪὸ οηᴚ, αċὸ ƀеɪηηе ƀυαɪὸ αɪη αn οłс ηе mαɪċ.

Chap. xiii.

1. Ďıoᴅ ʒać uıle anum uṁal ᴅo na cuṁaćᴅaıḃ acá óp a ćıonn. Oıp nı ḃ-ꝼuıl cuṁaćᴅa ap bıć aćᴅ ó Ḋhıa· aʒup na cuṁaćᴅa acá ann, ap o Ḋhıa ᴅo h-ópᴅuıʒeaᴅ ıaᴅ.

2. Cıp an aᴅḃappoın ʒıᴅ b'é ap bıć ćuıpeap a n-aʒaıᴅ a ćuṁaćᴅa, cuıpıᴅ pe a naʒaıᴅ opᴅaıʒe Ďe : aʒup an opeam ćuıpeap ıonna aʒaıᴅ ʒaḃaıᴅ ᴅamnuʒaᴅ ćuca ꝼeın.

3. Oıp ní ḃí eaʒla poıṁ uaćᴅapánáıḃ aıp pon ᴅeıʒníoṁapćaᴅ aćᴅ aıp pon ᴅpoıć [ʒníoṁapćaᴅ]. Uıme pın an mıan pıoc ḃeıć ʒan eaʒla an ćuṁaćᴅa opc? ᴅéan maıć, aʒup ᴅo ʒeaḃꝼa cú molaᴅ uaᴅ.

4. Oıp ap e peapḃꝛóʒancuıᴅe Ďe e ćum ᴅo ṁaıćeapapa. Cćᴅ ᴅá n-ᴅeapnaıᴅ cú olc, bıoᴅ eaʒla opc; oıp ní ʒo ᴅıoṁaoıneać ıomépap pe an cloıᴅeaṁ : oıp ap e peapḃꝛoʒancuıᴅe Ďé é, 'na ᴅıoʒalcóıp peıpʒe aıp an ce ᴅo ʒní olc.

5. Uıme pın ap éıʒean ḃeıć úṁal, ní [ᴅ'eaʒla] peıpʒe aṁáın, aćᴅ ꝼop aıp pon ćoınnpıaıp.

6. Oıp ıp uıme po íocap pıḃ cánacap: ᴅo ḃpıʒ ʒup peapḃꝛoʒancuıʒeaᴅa ᴅo Ḋhıa ıaᴅ, aʒ ᴅéanaᴅ a n-ᴅıććıll pa nıᴅ ćéaᴅna.

7. Cıp an aᴅḃappoın caḃpuıᴅ a n-ᴅualʒup ᴅo na huıle ᴅaoınıḃ : canaćup ᴅo'n ce [ᴅ'ap ᴅual] canaćup; cupᴅum ᴅo'n ce [ᴅ'ap ᴅual] cupᴅúm ; eaʒla pe pan ce [pe ap coıp] eaʒla ; onoıp ᴅo'n cé [ᴅ'ap coıp] onóıp.

8. Na bíoᴅ ꝼıaća aʒ aoın-neać opaıḃ, aćᴅ aṁaın pıḃ ꝼeın ᴅo ʒpaᴅuʒaᴅ a ćeıle: (oıp an cé ʒpáᴅaıʒeap a ćóṁappa ᴅo ćoıṁlíon pe an ᴅlıʒeaᴅ).

9. Oıp na [haıćeancapa], na ᴅean aᴅalcpannup, na ᴅeana ᴅunṁapḃaᴅ, na ᴅean ʒoıᴅ, na ᴅean ꝼıaᴅnuıpı

ḃnéiʒe, na ꝺeana naินṡ; aʒun ʒaċ aiṫne eile [ớa ḃ-ꝼuil ann], aṫáiꝺ ʒo haiṫʒeann ꝼá ḃníʒ an naiꝺ no, eaꝺon, ʒnaꝺaiʒ ꝺo ċoṁanna man ṫu ꝼein.

10. Ní ꝺeanann ʒnaꝺ olc ꝺo'n ċoṁannain : ain an aꝺ-ḃannoin [ané] an ʒnáꝺ coiṁlionaꝺ an ꝺlíʒe.

11, Aʒun nin, ne mean na h-aimnine, ʒun miṫiꝺ ꝺuinn anoin múnʒlaꝺ o ċoꝺlaꝺ : oin [in] ʒoine ꝺuin anoin an nlanuʒaꝺ na an uain ꝺo ċneiꝺeaman.

12. Ꝺo ċuaiꝺ an oiꝺċe ṫonainn aʒun ꝺo ớnuiꝺ an la ninn : uime nin ṫeilʒeam uainn oiḃneaċa an ꝺonċaꝺuin. Aʒun cuineam umainn eiꝺeaꝺ an ṫnolain.

13. Siuḃlam ʒo cuḃaiꝺ, aṁail na ló; ní a ʒ-cnaon na a meinʒe, na a neompaꝺoɩ́neaċꝺ na a macnuin, na a ʒ-ceannannaiċ na a ꝺ-ṫnúṫ.

14. Aċꝺ cuineꝺ umuiḃ an Ṫiʒeanna Íona Cniont, aʒun na bioꝺ cúnam na colla onaiḃ a mianʒunuiḃ.

IV.—1st *St. Peter*, ch. ii.

1. Uime nin ain ʒ-cun na h-uile ainʒiꝺeċꝺa, aʒun ṁeḃla, aʒun ꝼallnaċꝺ, aʒun ṫnúṫa, aʒun an uile iṫiompáiꝺ úaiḃ,

2. Man náoiꝺeanuiḃ nuaiꝺ-ḃeanṫa, bioꝺ ꝼonn aʒuiḃ a m-bainne ꝼionʒlan na ḃnéiṫne, ċum ḃeiṫ ớiḃ aʒ ꝼan nin;

3. Má ḃlaineaḃain cnéꝺ é míllne an Ṫiʒeanna.

4. An ṫí ċum a ḃ-ꝼuil niḃ an ꝺ-ṫeaċꝺ, noċ in cloċ beo, ꝺo ꝺiultaꝺ ʒo ꝺeiṁin ó ꝺáoiniḃ, aċꝺ aṫa ṫoʒṫa món-luáiꝺ, aʒ Ꝺia,

5. Aʒun biʒiớne man ḃéoċlocaiḃ, ṫoʒṫa núan ḃun ꝺ-ṫiʒ nnionaꝺálṫa, ḃun naʒantaċꝺ naoṁṫa, ċum ioꝺ-ḃanṫaꝺ nnionaꝺalṫa ꝺ'ꝼonáil, an a m-biaiꝺ ʒean aʒ Ꝺia ṫné Íona Cniont.

6. Uime ɼın ατα ɼʒɲıοϐέα ɼα ɼʒɲıοϐτuıɲ, ɼéuέ, cuıɲım α Sıon ppıoɱέloέ αn έuınne, τοʒέα, móɲlúαıὸ: αʒuɼ αn τe έɲeıɒeαɼ ınnτe nı ϐ-ɼuıʒe ɼe náıɼe.

7. Αıɼ αn αὸϐαɼɼon ατα ɼı 'nα honóıɼ οíϐɼe αʒα ϐ-ɼuıl cɼeıɒeαɱ: αέò ɒο'n οɼuınʒ ατα eαɼúɱαl, ɒο'n έloıc uɒ ɒο ὸıulταɒαɼ nα ɼαoıɼ, ɒο ɼınne cloέ έınn αn έuınne,

8. Αʒuɼ cloέ oılϐéıme, αʒuɼ cαɼɼuıc τuıɼlıὸ, ɒο'n οɼuınʒ ϐıoɼ eαɼuɱαl, ɒο ʒeıϐ oılϐéım ɼα'n m-bɼéıέıɼ; έum αɼ hóɼouıʒeαὸ ɼoɼ ıαɒ.

9. Αέò ıɼ cınéul τοʒέα ɼıϐɼe, ɼαʒαɼταέò ɼıoʒὸα, cıneαὸ nαoɱέα, pohαl αıɼ leıέ; ıonnuɼ ʒο ϐ-ɼoıllɼeoέαὸ ɼıϐ ɼuϐáılcıὸe αn τe ʒoıɼ ɼıϐ αɼ ɒoɼέαɒαɼ έum α ɼoluıɼ ıonʒαnτuıʒ ɼéın;

10. Ñoέ α nαllóò nαέ ɼαıϐ ϐuɼ b-pobαl, αέò αnoıɼ αɼ pobαl ɒο Ðhıα ɼıϐ: α òɲeαm nαέ ϐ-ɼuαıɼ τɼócαıɼe, ατα ɼıϐ αnoıɼ αıɼ ϐ-ɼáʒáıl τɼócαıɼe.

11. Α έáıɼɒe ʒɼáɒαέ, .ıαɼɼuım ɒ'αέέuınʒe [οɼuıϐ], mαɼ òeoɼuıòıϐ αʒuɼ oılıέɼıϐ, ɼıϐ ɼéın ɒο ɼeαέnαὸ αɼ αınɱıαnuıϐ nα colnα, noέ ϐıoɼ αʒ cατέuʒαὸ α n-αʒuıὸ α n'αnmα.

12. Ðíoὸ ɒeαʒέoınϐeαɼɼáıɒ αʒuıϐ α meαɼʒ nα ʒ-Cıneαὸαέ: ıonnαɼ α n-áıτ αn ıέıomɼáıὸ ɒο ʒníò οɼuıϐ mαɼ luέò míʒɼníoɱ, ʒο mαὸ héıoıɼ ɼıu, αɼ nα ɒeαʒoıϐɲıϐ ɒο έíɼıɒ ɼıαɒ, ʒlóıɼ ɒο έαϐαıɼτ ɒο Ðhıα ɼα lá 'nα ϐ-ɼeuέɼuıὸ οɼɼέα.

13. [Uıme ɼın] bíʒıὸ úɱαl ɒα ʒαέ uıle óɲɒαıʒέe òαonὸα, αɼ ɼon αn Cıʒeαɼnα: nı he αmáın ɒο'n ɼıʒ, mαɼ αn τé αʒα ϐ-ɼuıl áıɼoέeαnnαɼ.

14. Αέò ɒο nα h-uαέɒαɼánuıϐ [mαɼ αn ʒ-céαɒnα], mαɼ αn luέò cuıɼέeαɼ uαὸ έum ɒíoʒαlτuıɼ αɼ luέò nα míʒɼníoɱ, αʒuɼ έum molτα luέò nα n-ɒéıʒʒníoɱ.

15. Oıɼ ıɼ mαɼ ɼın, αʒ ɒéαnαὸ mαıέeαɼα òíϐ, αɼ τoıl le Ðıα ɼɼıαn ɒο έuɼ ɼe h-αınϐɼıoɼ nα n-ɒαoıneαὸ éıʒceılлıὸe.

16. Maꝑ [óaoıne] ꝛaoꝛa, aᵹuꝛ nı maꝑ an oꝛuınᵹ aᵹa b-ꝛuıl an τ-ꝛaoıꝛꝛe 'na bꝛaτ ꝛoluıóⱒe an uılc, aⱄo maꝑ ꝛeaꝛbꝛóᵹanτuıᵹıóe Oe.

17. Cuᵹuıó onóıꝑ oo na huıle [óaoınıb]. ᵹꝛaóuıᵹe na oeaꝛbꝛaıꝛe. óıoó eaᵹla Oe oꝛuıb. Cuᵹuıó onóıꝑ oo'n ꝛıᵹ.

18. A ꝛeaꝛbꝛóᵹanτuıᵹıó, [bıᵹıó] uṁal oa [buꝑ] maıᵹ-ıꝛτꝛıb maılle pıꝑ an uıle ꝛaıτⱄeaꝑ ; nı he aṁaın oo na [maıᵹıꝛτꝛıb] maıⱒe oeaᵹⱄꝛoıóeaⱄa, aⱄo ꝛóꝑ oo na oꝛoⱄ [ṁaıᵹıꝛτꝛıb].

19. Oıꝑ (ıꝑ) nıó ꝛo ıꝑ ꝛıu buıóeaⱄaꝑ o'a n-ıomⱄꝛuıó neaⱄ ooılᵹeaꝑ aıꝑ ꝛon coınnꝛıaıꝑ oo ⱄaob Oe, aᵹ ꝛulanᵹ na h-eaᵹⱄóꝛa.

20. Oıꝑ cꝛeuo [é] maꝑ áóbaꝑ molτa o'a n-ıomⱄꝛa ꝛıb ᵹo ꝛóıᵹıoeⱄ ᵹabáıl oo óóꝛnuıb oꝛuıb aıꝑ n-oeanaṁ ꝛeacuıó óıb? aⱄo, o'a b-ꝛuılnᵹe ꝛıb ᵹo ꝛoıᵹıoeaⱄ, aᵹuꝑ ꝛıb aᵹ oeanaó maıⱒeaꝛa, [aꝑ nıó] ꝛın [o'a bꝛuıl] Oıa buıóeaⱄ.

21. Oıꝑ ıꝑ ⱄuıᵹe ꝛo ꝛóꝑ oo ᵹoıꝛeaó ꝛıb: oıꝑ oo ꝛulluınᵹ Cꝛıoꝛτ maꝑ an ᵹ-ceaona aıꝑ aꝑ ꝛoınne aᵹ ꝛáᵹbaıl ꝛompla aᵹuınn, ıonnuꝑ ᵹo leanꝛaó ꝛıb a loꝛᵹ ;

22. An τe naⱄ oeaꝛnuıó ꝛeacaó, aᵹuꝑ aᵹ naⱄ ꝛꝛıⱄ meabaıl 'na béal ;

23. An τe naⱄ oeaꝛnuıó an-ⱄaınτ, a naᵹuıó na h-an-ⱄaınτe oo ꝛınneaó aıꝑ; naⱄ oeaꝛnuıó baᵹaꝑ, aᵹ ꝛulanᵹ óo ; aⱄo τuᵹ [é ꝛéın] a láıṁ an τe oo ᵹnı bꝛeıⱒeaṁnuꝑ ᵹo ceaꝑτ :

24. An τe o'ıomⱄaıꝑ aꝑ b-peacuıᵹne ann a ⱄoꝛꝛ ꝛéın aıꝑ an ᵹ-cꝛann, ıonnuꝑ aıꝑ m-beıⱒ óuınne maꝑb oo na ꝛeacuıᵹıb, ᵹo maıꝛꝛemıꝑ oo'n ꝛıꝛeanτaⱄo : an τe aᵹ aꝑ leıᵹeaꝛaó ꝛıbꝛe ꝛe na ⱄꝛeuⱄouıb.

25. Oıꝑ oo babaıꝑ maꝑ ⱄaoꝛⱄuıb aıꝑ ꝛeaⱄꝛáın ; aⱄo anoıꝛ oo ꝛılleaó ꝛıb ᵹo h-Aoóaıꝛe aᵹuꝑ ᵹo h-Eaꝛboᵹ buꝑ n-anman.

THE CHURCH CATECHISM.

ceaȝasȝ crᴉosoaᴉȝhe,

Eaóon leᴉȝᴉonn aʀ ᴉonꝝoȝloméa oo ȝaċ uᴉle óuᴉne ꝛul
ʀaċꝛuʀ ꝝaoᴉ laᴉ́ꝝ Eaʀboᴉc.

Ceᴉʀᴁ. Cʀeuo e h-aᴉnmʀe.

Ꝝʀ. Ꞁ no ꝿ.

Ce. Ce ċuȝ an ᴁ-aᴉnmʀᴉ óuᴉᴁ ?

Ꝝʀ. ꝿo Ꝺhᴉa-aᴉéʀe aȝuʀ mo Ꝺhᴉa-ꝿ́áᴉéʀe ann mo
baᴉʀoeaó, anna n-oeaʀnaó óᴉom ball oo Chʀᴉoʀo, leanb
Ꝺe, aȝuʀ oᴉȝ́ʀe ʀᴉoȝáċᴁa neᴉ́ꝝe.

Ce. Cʀeuo oo ʀᴉnneaoaʀ oo óᴉa-aᴉéʀe aȝuʀ oo óᴉa-
ꝿ́aᴉéʀe an ᴁ-an ʀᴉn aᴉʀ oo ꝛonʀa?

Ꝝʀ. Ꝺo ȝ́eallaoaʀ aȝuʀ oo ꝿ́oᴉoᴉȝeaoaʀ ᴁʀᴉ neᴉ́ċe ann
m'aᴉnm, a ȝ-ceaooᴉʀ, ȝo n-oᴉulᴁʀaᴉnn oo'n oᴉabal aȝuʀ
o'á oᴉbʀeaċaᴉb uᴉle, oo ꝛoᴉmʀ, aȝuʀ oo óᴉoꝿ́aoᴉneaʀ an
oʀoċꝛaoȝaᴉlʀe, aȝuʀ oo ȝaċ uᴉle aᴉnꝿ́ᴉanaᴉb ʀeacaóaċa
na colna. Cln oaʀa h-uaᴉʀ ȝo ȝ-cʀeᴉoꝛᴉnn ȝaċ uᴉle aᴉʀᴁᴉo-
ȝal oo'n ċʀeᴉoeaꝿ́ Chʀᴉoʀoaᴉóe. Clȝuʀ a ᴁʀeaʀ uaᴉʀ, ȝo
ȝ-coᴉꝿ́eaoꝛuᴉnn ᴁoᴉl naoꝿ́éa aȝuʀ aᴉċeanᴁa Ꝺe, aȝuʀ ȝo
ʀᴉoboluᴉnn ᴉonnᴁa ᴁʀé uᴉle laeċᴉb mo beaċa.

Ce. Ꞁaċ meaʀaᴉʀ ȝo b-ꝝuᴉl o'ꝛᴉaċaᴉb oʀᴁ a ċʀeᴉoeaꝿ́
aȝuʀ a óeanaꝿ́ maʀ oo ȝ́eallaoaʀ aʀ oo ꝛon?

Ꝝʀ. ꝿeaʀuᴉm ȝo oeᴉ́ꝝᴉn; aȝuʀ le ᴁoᴉl Ꝺe, oéanꝛa me
maʀ ʀᴉn. Clȝuʀ beᴉʀᴉm buᴉóeacuʀ ó ċʀoᴉóe o'áʀ n-Claaᴉʀ
neaꝿ́óa, ꝛa maʀ oo ȝoᴉʀ oʀm ċum na ʀᴁaᴉoeʀe an ᴁ-ʀla-
nuᴉȝ́ċe, ᴁʀe ᴉoʀa Cʀᴉoʀᴁ aʀ Slánaᴉȝ́ċeoᴉʀ. Clȝuʀ ȝuᴉóᴉm
Ꝺᴉa ȝʀaʀa oo ċabaᴉʀᴁ óaꝿ́ ċoꝿ́naᴉȝ́e 'ʀan ʀᴁaᴉo ċeaona
ȝo cʀᴉ́ċ mo beaċa.

Ce. Aiṫíɼ aiɼcioʒail ɗo ċɼeíoiṁ.

Fɼ. Cɼeíoim a n-Ðia an t-Aṫaiɼ uile-ċuṁaċɗaċ, cɼuṫ-uíʒṫeoiɼ neíṁe aʒuɼ talṁan: aʒuɼ a n-Íoɼa Cɼíoɼt aon ṁacɼan aɼ ɗ-Tiʒeaɼna, ɗo ʒaḃaɗ ó'n Spíoɼaɗ naoṁ, ɗo ɼuʒaɗ leíɼ an óiʒ Muíɼe, ɗ'ꝼulaínʒ páiɼ ꝼaoí Phoínt Phíoláíɗ, ɗo ceuɼaɗ, ɗo ꝼuaíɼ báɼ aʒuɼ ɗo h-aɗlaíceaɗ; ċuaíɗ ɼíoɼ ʒo h-íɼíoɼn, ɗ'eíɼʒíɗ aɼíɼ an tɼeaɼ la ó na maɼḃaíḃ, ɗo ċuaíɗ ɼuaɼ aɼ neaṁ, aʒuɼ ata na ɼuíɗe aɼ láiṁ ɗeíɼ Ðe an Aṫaɼ uile-ċuṁaċɗaíʒ; aɼ ɼín tíucꝼa ɼe ɗo ḃɼeíṫ bɼeíṫe aɼ beoɗaíḃ aʒuɼ aɼ ṁaɼḃaíḃ. Cɼeíoim ɼan Spíoɼaɗ naoṁṫa; a naoíṁ Eaʒluíɼ ċatoílíce; cuṁáoín na naoṁ; maíṫeaṁ na b-peacaíʒe; eíɼeíɼʒe na colna, aʒuɼ an beaṫa ṁaɼṫanaċ. Amen.

Ce. Cɼéaɗ ɗo níòíɼ ɗ'ꝼoʒluím ʒo haíɼíʒe annɼ 'na h-aiɼcioʒail ɼe ɗo ċɼeíoiṁ?

Fɼ. A ʒ-céaɗóíɼ, ꝼoʒlamaím ċɼeíoeaṁ a n-Ðia an t-Aṫaiɼ, ɗo ċɼuṫuíʒ me ꝼein, aʒuɼ an ɼaoʒal uile.

An ɗaɼa h-uaíɼ, cɼeíoeaṁ a n-Ðia an Mac ɗ-ꝼuáɼʒaíl me, aʒuɼ an cíneaɗ ɗaonna uíle.

An tɼeaɼ uaíɼ, cɼeíoeaṁ a n-Ðia an Spíoɼaɗ naoṁṫa ɗo naoṁaíɗ me, aʒuɼ pohal toʒṫa Ðe uíle.

Ce. A ouḃɼaíɼ ʒuɼ ʒeallaɗaɼ ɗo Ðia-aiɼpe aʒuɼ ɗo Ðia-ṁáiɼpe aɼ ɗo ɼon ʒo ʒ-coíṁeaɗꝼá aiṫeanɗa Ðe. Iníɼ òaṁ cía a líon?

Fɼ. A ɗeíc.

Ce. Cɼeuɗ íaɗ ɼín?

Fɼeaʒɼa. An ceaɗna ɗo laḃaíɼ Ðia 'ɼan b-ꝼíceaɗ caíbíoíl ɗ'Ecɼoɗuɼ, aʒ ɼaɗ. Iɼ míɼí an Tiʒeaɼna ɗo Ðhía, noċ ɗo ċɼeoɼuíʒ ṫuɼa amaċ aɼ talaṁ na h-Eʒíɼte, aɼ tíʒ na ɗaoíɼɼe.

I. Ní ḃíaíɗ Ðia aɼ bíṫ eíle aʒaɗ am láṫaíɼɼe.

II. Ní ɗeanɼa tu ɗuít ꝼein íoṁaíʒ aɼ bíṫ ʒɼaḃalta, nó coɼaṁlaċṫ aon neíṫe, ata a b-ꝼlaíṫíoɼ ɼuaɼ, no ɼa

ċalaṁ ṗioṗ, no ann ṛa n-uıṛʒe ꝼaoı an ċalaṁ, nı ċlaonꝛa
ċu ṛıoṛ ċuca, nı aȯṗoċaıṗ ıaȯ: oıṗ mıṗı an Cıʒeaṗna ȯo
Ꝺhıa, ıṗ Ꝺıa euȯṁaṗ me, ċıʒ ȯ'ꝼeuċaın ṗeacaıȯ na
n-aıċṗeaċ aṗ an ʒ-cloınn ʒuṗ an ċṗeaṗ, aʒuṗ an ceaċṗa-
ṁaȯ ʒlún ȯo'n oṗoınʒ ꝼuaċuıʒeaṗ me, aʒuṗ ċaıṗbeanaım
ċṗócaıṗe ȯo ṁílċıḃ ȯo'n luċċ a ʒṛaȯuıʒeaṗ me, aʒuṗ
a ċoıṁeaȯaṗ m'aıċeanċa.

III. Nı ċaıbeoṗaıṗ aınm an Cıʒeaṗna ȯo Ꝺhıa ʒo
ȯıoṁaoın: oıṗ nı ṁeaṛꝼuıȯ an Cıʒeaṗna an ċe ȯo ḃeıċ
neıṁċıonċaċ ȯo ḃeıṗ a aınm ʒo ȯıoṁaoın.

IV. Cuıṁnıʒ la na Saḃóıȯe ȯo ċonʒṁaıl naoṁċa. Se
laeċe ṛaoıṗeoċaṗ ċu, aʒuṗ ȯéanꝼuıṗ a ḃ-ꝼuıl aʒaȯ le
ȯeanaṁ, aċȯ ıṗe an ṛeaċċṁaȯ la Saḃoıȯ an Cıʒeaṗna
ȯo Ꝺhıa, nı ȯeana ċu oḃaıṗ aṗ bıċ ann, ċu ꝼeın, aʒuṗ
ȯo ṁac, aʒuṗ ȯ'ınʒean, ċ'óʒlaċ, aʒuṗ ȯo ḃanóʒlaċ, ċ'eallaċ, aʒuṗ an coıṁıʒċeaċ aċa ċaoḃ ıṛċıʒ ȯoċ ȯoıṗṛıḃ:
oıṗ ȯo ṗınne an Cıʒeaṗna a ṛe laeċıḃ neaṁ aʒuṗ ċalaṁ,
an ꝼaıṗʒe, aʒuṗ an uıle nıȯ aċá ıonċa, aʒuṗ ȯo ċoṁnaıȯ
ṛe an ṛeaċċṁaȯ la: uıme ṛın ȯo ḃeannuıʒ an Cıʒeaṗna
la na Saḃóıȯe aʒaṗ ȯo naoṁuıʒ e.

V. Onoṗuıʒ ċ'aċaıṗ aʒuṗ ȯo ṁaċaıṗ, ıonnuṗ ʒo
m-baȯ ꝼaȯa ȯo laeċe aṗ an ȯ-ċalaṁ noċ ȯo ḃeıṗ an
Cıʒeaṗna ȯo Ꝺhıa ȯuıċ

VI. Nı ȯéana ċu ȯúnṁaṗḃaȯ.

VII. Nı ȯéana ċu aȯalċṗannaṗ.

VIII. Nı ȯéana ċu ʒoıȯ.

IX. Nı ḃéaṗa ċu ꝼıaȯnuıṗe ḃṗeıðe a n-aʒaıȯ ȯo ċoṁaṗṛan.

X. Nı ꝼaınċeoċa ċu ċıʒ ȯo ċoṁaṗṛan, nı ꝼaınċeoċa
ċu bean ȯo comaṗṛan, no oʒlaȯ ȯo ċoṁaṗṛan, no a
ḃanóʒlaċ, no a ȯaṁ, no a aṛal, no ennı ıṗ le ȯo ċoṁ-
aṗṛaın.

Ce. Cṙeuⱱ ⱱo ꝥnı ᴄu ⱱ'ꝼoᵹlaım ᵹoⸯꞃꝑeꞃıalᴄa le n-a h-aıᴄeanᴄaıḃꞃe ?

Fꞃ. Ꝼoᵹlamaım ȯa nıȯ ; mo ȯualᵹuꞃ ⱱo Ɗhıa, aᵹuꞃ mo ȯualᵹuꞃ ⱱom ċoṁaꞃꞃaın.

Ce. Cꞃéaⱱ e ⱱo ȯualᵹuꞃ ⱱo Ɗhıa ?

Fꞃ. 'Se mo ȯualᵹuꞃ ⱱo Ɗhıa cꞃeıⱱeaṁ ann, eaᵹla ḃeıċ oꞃm ꞃoıṁe, a ᵹꞃaȯuᵹaȯ le mo ċꞃoıȯe uıle, le m'ınnᴄınn uıle, le m'anam uıle, aᵹuꞃ le mo neaꞃᴄ uıle ; a aȯꞃaȯ, buıȯeaċuꞃ ⱱo ċaḃaıꞃᴄ ⱱó, mo ȯoıᵹ uıle ⱱo ċuꞃ ann, ᵹaıꞃm aıꞃ, a aınm naoṁᴄa aᵹuꞃ a ꝼoᴄal ⱱ'onoꞃaȯ ; aᵹuꞃ ꞃeıꞃḃıꞃ ⱱo ȯeanaṁ ᵹo ꝼıꞃꞃıneaċ ⱱo aꞃ ꝼeaȯ mo ḃeaċa uıle.

Ce. Ᵹo ⱱe ⱱo ȯualᵹuꞃ ⱱoᴄ ċoṁaꞃꞃaın ?

Fꞃ. Aꞃe mo ȯualᵹuꞃ ⱱom ċoṁaꞃꞃaın, a ᵹꞃaȯuᵹaȯ maꞃ me ꝼeın, aᵹuꞃ ⱱeanaṁ ⱱo na huıle ȯaoınıḃ maꞃ ba ṁıan leam ıaⱱ ⱱo ȯeanaṁ ȯam. Ṁ'aċaıꞃ aᵹuꞃ mo ṁáċaıꞃ ⱱo ᵹꞃaȯuᵹaȯ, ⱱ'onóꞃaȯ, aᵹaꞃ ȯ'ꝼoꞃᴄaċᴄ. Onóıꞃ aᵹuꞃ uṁlaċⱱ ⱱo ᴄaḃaıꞃᴄ ⱱo'n Rıᵹ, aᵹuꞃ ⱱ'a ḃꝼuıl a ᵹ-ceannaꞃ ꝼaaı. Me ꝼeın ⱱ'uṁluᵹaȯ ⱱom uıle ꞃᴄıuꞃuıᵹċeoıꞃıḃ, ċeaᵹaꞃᵹċoıꞃıḃ, aoȯaıꞃıḃ ꞃꞃıoꞃaȯalᴄa aᵹuꞃ ṁaıᵹıꞃᴄꞃıḃ. Me ꝼeın ⱱ'ıomċaꞃ ᵹo h-uıꞃıꞃıol, aᵹuꞃ ᵹo h-uꞃꞃamaċ ⱱo ᵹaċ uıle ȯuıne aꞃ ꝼeaꞃꞃ na me ꝼéın. Ᵹan ⱱıoᵹḃáıl a ȯeanaṁ ⱱ'aoıneaċ le bꞃéıċıꞃ na le ᵹnıoṁ. Ȯheıċ ꝼıꞃınneaċ aᵹuꞃ ceaꞃᴄ an m'uıle ċonnꞃaȯ. Ᵹan maıłıꞃ na ꝼuaċ ḃeıċ an mo ċꞃoıȯe. Ṁo laṁa ⱱo ċonᵹṁaıl o ꞃıocaȯ aᵹuꞃ o ᵹoıⱱ, aᵹuꞃ mo ċeanᵹa o ȯꞃoċċaınᴄ, o bꞃéıᵹ, aᵹuꞃ o ꞃᵹannaıl. Ṁo ċaꞃꞃ ⱱo ċonᵹṁaıl a meaꞃaꞃȯaċᴄ, a ꞃoꞃꞃaıȯeaċᴄ, aᵹuꞃ a n-ᵹeanmnaıᵹeaċᴄ. Ᵹan maoın ⱱaoıneaȯ eıle ⱱo ꝼanᴄuᵹaȯ na ⱱ'ıaꞃꞃaȯ ; aċᴄ ꝼoᵹlaım aᵹuꞃ ꞃaoċaꞃ ⱱo ȯeanaṁ ċum mo ḃeaċa ⱱ'ꝼáᵹaıl ᵹo cneaꞃⱱa, aᵹuꞃ ⱱeanaṁ maꞃ ıꞃ ⱱual ȯaṁ ann ꞃa ꞃᴄaıⱱ ḃeaċa ꞃın ċum aꞃ mıan le Ɗıa mo ᵹaıꞃm.

Ce. Ṁo leınıḃ ṁaıċ, bıoȯ a ꝼıoꞃ ꞃo aᵹaⱱ, naċ ḃ-ꝼuıl

ap oo cumap na neiċepe oo óeanaṁ uaiċ ḟein, na
piobal a n-aiċeanċaiḃ De aȝup peipḃip oo óeanaṁ óo,
ȝan a ȝnápa ppepialċapan, aip a ȝ-caiċḟip poȝlaim
ȝaipm oo óeanaṁ ȝaċ uile am le h-upnaiȝ óuċpaċċaiȝ,
uime pin léiȝ óam a ċlop, an ḃ-ḟeaouip opáio an Ċiȝeapna oo paó.

Ḟpe. Ap n-Aċaip a ċa ap neaṁ, naoṁċap h-ainm.
Ċiȝeaó oo pioȝaċo. Deanċap oo ċoil ap an ċalaṁ, map
níċeap ap neaṁ. Ċaḃaip óúinn anoiu ap n-apán laeċea-
ṁuil. Aȝup maiċ óúinn ap ȝ-cionċa, map ṁaiċmíone
óóiḃ oo cionċaiȝeap 'n ap n-aȝaió. Aȝup na ċpeópuiȝ
inn ċum caċaiȝċe ; aċo paop inn o olc. Amen.

Ce. Cpeao iappaip aip Dhia pa n-upnaiȝpe ?

Ḟp. Iappaim aip mo Ċhiȝeapna Dia ap n-Aċaip
neaṁóa, ċioólaicċeoip ȝaċ uile ṁaiċip, a ȝpapa oo
ċup ċuȝam ḟein, aȝup ċum ȝaċ uile óuine, ċum ȝo n-óea-
nam aópaó óo, peipḃip óo, aȝup uṁlaċo oo, map ap cóip
óúinn. Aȝup ȝuióim Dia ȝaċ uile neiċe oo ċaḃaipċ
óúinn aċa piaċóanaċ o'ap n-anmannaiḃ mapáon aȝup
oap ȝ-coppuiḃ ; aȝup ȝo m-beiċ pe ċpocaipeaċ óuinn,
aȝup ȝo maiċḟeaó óúinn ap ḃ-peacaióe ; aȝup ȝo m-baó
i a ċoil ap pábáil, aȝup ap ȝ-copainċ ann ȝaċ uile ċon-
ċaḃaipċ ppiopaio aȝup colna : aȝup ȝo ȝ-cuiṁoeoċaó
inn o ȝaċ uile ḟeacaó, aȝup ṁoploċċaiḃ, aȝup o'p
naṁaio ppiopaoalċa aȝup o ḃap ḟioppaióe. Aȝup aċa
ooiȝ aȝam ȝo n-óeana po o'a ċpocaipe, aȝap o'a ṁaiċeap,
ċpe ap o-Ċiȝeapna Iopa Cpiopċ, aȝup ap an aóḃap pin
oeipim, Amen. Ȝo paiḃ map pin.

Ceipċ. Cia lion Sacpaimenċeaó oo opouiȝ Cpiopo
an Eaȝluip?

Ḟp. Dha Shacpaimeinċ aṁáin aċa ȝo ȝeneapalċa
piaċċanaċ ċum planuiȝċe, eaóon, óaipċeaó, aȝup Sui-
péap an Ċiȝeapna.

Ce. Cpeaꝺ ꞇuiᵹıpe leıp an ḃ-ꝼocalpa Sacpaımenꞇ?

Ꝼp. Ꞇuıᵹım coṁapꞇa ꝼoıpımıollaċ poꝼaıcpı ᵹṕáp ınnṁeoꝺonaċ aᵹup ᵹpıopaꝺalꞇa ꞇaḃaıpꞇe ꝺuınn, ꝺo opouıᵹ Cpıopꞇ ꝼeın, map ṕlıᵹe le ḃ-ꝼaᵹamaoıꝺ na ᵹpapa ceaꝺna, aᵹup map ᵹeall ċum a n-ꝺeapḃꞇa ꝺuınn.

Ce. Ca ṁeıꝺ pann a Sacpaımeınꞇ?

Ꝼp. Ꝺha pann : an coṁapꞇa ꝼoıpımıollaċ poꝼaıcpe, aᵹup ᵹpapa ınṁeoꝺonaċ Spıopaꝺalꞇa.

Ce. Cpeaꝺ e coṁapꞇa ꝼoıpımıollaċ no ꝼoıpm a ḃaıp-ꝺıꝺ?

Ꝼp. Uıpᵹe, ann a m-baıpꝺeap a peappa a n-aınm an-Aꞇap, aᵹup an ṁıc aᵹup an Spıopaıꝺ naoıṁ.

Ceıpꞇ. Cpeaꝺ ı an ᵹpap ınnṁeoꝺonaċ aᵹup ᵹpıopaꝺalꞇa?

Ꝼp. Ꝺáp ċum peacaıꝺ, aᵹup aıꞇᵹeın ᵹo ꝼıpeanꞇaċꞇ; óıp ap m-beıꞇ ꝺuınn ó naꝺuıp beıpꞇe a ḃ-peacaꝺ, aᵹup 'n ap ᵹ-cloınn ꝺıḃꝼeıpᵹe, ꝺeanꞇap leıp po clann na n-ᵹpáp ꝺınn.

Ce. Cpeaꝺ ıappꞇap ap peappannaıḃ a ḃıap ċum a m-baıpꞇe?

Ꝼp. Aıꞇpıᵹe le a ꝺ-ꞇpeıᵹıꝺ peacaꝺ : aᵹup cpeıꝺeaṁ, le ᵹ-cpeıꝺıꝺ ᵹo ꝺıonᵹṁalꞇa ᵹeallaṁna Ꝺe ꝺeanꞇap ꝺóıḃ 'pan ꞇ-pacpaımeınꞇ ꝺo.

Ce. Maıpeaꝺ cpeaꝺ uıme a m-baıpꝺeap leınıḃ, an ꞇan ꞇpe na n-oıᵹe naċ ḃ-ꝼeaꝺuıꝺ ıaꝺ pın ꝺo ċoıṁlıonaꝺ?

Ꝼp. Ap an aꝺḃap ᵹo n-ᵹeallaıꝺ ıaꝺ apaon le na m-bannaıᵹ; aᵹup aꞇa ꝺ'ꝼıaċaıḃ oppꞇa ꝼeın, an ꞇ-an ċıocꝼuıꝺ ċum áoıpe, an ᵹeallaṁ pın ꝺo ċoıṁlíonaꝺ.

Ce. Cpeaꝺ ꝼa'p h-opouıᵹeaꝺ Sacpaımeınꞇ ꝼuıpeıp an Ꞇıᵹeapna?

Ꝼp. Chum ᵹnaꞇċuıṁne ıoꝺḃapꞇa ḃáıp Chpıopꞇ, aᵹup na ꞇaıpbe ꝺo ᵹeıḃmıꝺ ꝺ'a ḃpıᵹ.

Ce. Cpeaꝺ e an pann ꝼoıpımeallaċ, no coṁapꞇa, ꝼuıpeıp an Ꞇıᵹeapna?

Ḟp. Apán aᵹup ṗíon, ꝺo aiėnıꝺ an Ꞇıᵹeapna ꝺo ᵹlacaꝺ.

Ce. Cpeaꝺ e an pann ınnṁeoꝺonaė, no an nıꝺ ꝺo ėoṁapėaıᵹeap leo?

Ḟp. Copp aᵹup ꝼuıl Chpıopꞇ, ꝺo ᵹlacꞇap aᵹup ᵹaḃėap ᵹo ꝺeıṁın aᵹup ᵹo ꝺeapḃėa le na cpeıꝺṁıꝺ a ꝼuıpeap an Ꞇıᵹeapna.

Ce. Cpeaꝺ ıaꝺ na ꞇaıpḃeaꝺa ꝺa n-ꝺeanꞇap pannṗaıpꞇeaė pınn leıp an ꞇ-pacpaımeınꞇpe?

Ḟp. Neapꞇuᵹaꝺ aᵹup beaėuᵹaꝺ ap n-anman le copp aᵹup le ꝼuıl Chpıopꞇ, aṁaıl map neapꞇuıᵹėeap aᵹup beoᵹuıꝺėeap ap ᵹ-cuıpp leıp an apán aᵹup a ḃ-ṗíon.

Ce. Cpeaꝺ ıappėap ap an ꝺpuınᵹ ꝺo ėıᵹ ėum puıpeıp an Ꞇıᵹeapna?

Ḟp. Iaꝺ ꝼeın ꝺo pcpuꝺaꝺ, an ḃ-ꝼuıl aıėpeaėap ꝼıpınneaė oppėa pa na b-peacaıꝺe ꝺo pınneaꝺap, aᵹ cup pompa ᵹo ꝺıonᵹṁalꞇa beaėa nuaꝺ ꝺo ėaıėeaṁ, aᵹup cpeıꝺeaṁ peapṁaė ꝺo ḃeıė aca a ꝺ-ꞇpocaıpe Ꝺe, ꞇpe Chpíopꞇ, le cuıṁne ḃuıꝺıᵹ a ḃáıp, aᵹup a ḃeıė a ᵹ-capėannaėꞇ le ᵹaė uıle ꝺuıne.

THE END.

In the Press, and shortly will be published, in 8vo.,

A

GRAMMAR OF THE IRISH LANGUAGE,

FOR

𝕿𝖍𝖊 𝖀𝖘𝖊 𝖔𝖋 𝖙𝖍𝖊 𝕾𝖙𝖚𝖉𝖊𝖓𝖙𝖘

IN

THE COLLEGE OF ST. COLUMBA.

By JOHN O'DONOVAN, Esq.

Dublin: HODGES AND SMITH, Grafton-street, Booksellers to the
University.

CPSIA information can be obtained
at www.ICGtesting.com
Printed in the USA
LVOW04s1531311016
511026LV00042B/1601/P